This
Baby Name Book
is for

_____

The Most Unique Baby Names Ever!

17,000 Names Included in this Book!

# THERE'S Magic IN YOUR NAME

## MARTY WILSON

Miracle PUBLISHING

Published by:

Miracle
PUBLISHING

Martykwilson@aol.com
Phone: 888-660-0277
Fax: (360) 898-7003
80 East Ridgecrest Drive
Union, Washington 98592

Printed and bound by Gorham Printing
Rochester, Washington
Cover and text design by Kathy Campbell
Edited by BJ Fandrich

ISBN 0-9767428-0-2
Library of Congress Control Number: 2005925246

First Edition, First Printing
Printed in the United States of America

## PUBLISHER'S NOTE

I dedicate my book to my three children,
Season MacKenzie, Story Landon and Salem Chase

You're all the love of my life
and the incentive for writing this book.

—Mom

I'd like to thank my dear friend Judy Berrian for all her
countless hours and her support for the past twenty-five years.
To my clients, family, friends and associates at Olympia Pediatrics

Thanks to Mom for always being there for me

To my two best friends Barb and Lorraine for all your support !

Most of all I'd like to thank my husband Brad
for all his encouragement and believing in me.
Thank you with all my heart,

God bless you all. Love you,

—Marty

# ★ CONTENTS ★

# There's *Magic* in Your Name

There are over 25,000,000 pregnant women right now. What in the world will all these new parents name their babies? The children of the twenty-first century will need exciting and unique names!

There are many baby name books on the market; however, they are almost entirely composed of traditional names. But today's parents are in search of names that are creative and inspiring. *There's Magic in Your Name* stimulates your imagination and inspires you to create your own magical name for your child.

I have probably named enough babies to populate a small city. It started in my beauty salon approximately twenty-five years ago. My clients loved my children's names—Season, Story, and Salem—and called me for advice about their own baby names. Parents have even contacted me from the hospital, desperate to find a magical name for their little bundle of joy!

I have collected over 17,000 names during twenty-five years of research and hard work. You will find a mix of common and uncommon names for every

individual's preference. Some names are familiar, many have a twist in spelling, but most of the names in this book are creative and unique. I have called on many sources from around the world, such as: birth records, atlases, phone books, pediatricians, celebrities, friends, and family.

Since many of these names can be used for either sex, this book has not been divided into sections based on gender. As you will see, a change in pronunciation, a vowel, or another letter can transform the name entirely, making it impossible to categorize.

The first and most important gift you will give to your child is the gift of a magical name. Remember, a name is forever and will last a lifetime!

As a *special bonus* we have included a Pregnancy Journal in this book. This is a wonderful diary to keep track of all the details you do not want to forget about your pregnancy (including pages for pictures of you and Baby as you grow!).

—Marty Wilson

★ "In the Hebrew Tradition,
a name is given to a person
to describe one's Character"

I love this practice. Even Jesus changed the names of the people he met to describe the character of that person. So why do we think we have to choose a name before our babies are born? That's great if you do, but if you don't have a name picked out in time, don't worry.

Please do not feel pressured to choose a name right away. Parents think they have to settle on a name before the baby is born, and that's just not true. For instance, my son Story was supposed to be "Dallas Story" before he was born. When it came time to fill out the birth certificate, I looked into his eyes, and just at that moment he looked like a Story Landon.

Sometimes I've found that you really do need to see your baby and his or her personality before choosing. It's great if you choose one and it fits right away, but if it doesn't, I promise it will come to you. Once I had a friend who didn't name her baby for three months after she brought him home!

It's a good idea to take notes of all the names you've gathered and save your favorites. You can do this in the Pregnancy Journal in the back of this book. This will help you weed through the ones that just don't click. What really matters is for

you to love the name. Sometimes you have to repeat it over and over until it sounds familiar. Take your time, be creative, and search for that magical name that will fit perfectly.

One other thing I would suggest is not to take it personally if someone doesn't like the name you choose. That's very common and one reason that there are baby name books with thousands of names.

It's meant to be a fun time, so I hope you enjoy yourself. I wish you all the luck and happy searching!

Lullabies are calming and wonderful. Here are some standard lullabies, and you can find many more on CDs and tapes. I've included a song I wrote for my children and sang to them every morning to wake them up. They laugh about it now but also loved it. They say someday they'll sing it to their children.

## DAY IS DONE

Day is done, gone the sun,
From the lake, from the hills, from the sky.
All is well, safely rest,
God is nigh

### ROCK-A-BYE BABY
Rock-a-bye baby, in the treetop
When the wind blows, the cradle will rock
When the bough breaks, the cradle will fall
And down will come baby, cradle and all.


### ALL THROUGH THE NIGHT
Sleep my child and peace attend thee,
All through the night
Guardian angels God will send thee,
All through the night
Soft the drowsy hours are creeping,
Hill and dale in slumber sleeping
I my loved ones' watch am keeping,
All through the night.

### WAKE-UP LULLABY (by Marty Wilson)
Wake up, wake up you sleepyhead
Get up, get up, get out of bed
No kid of mine, come rain or shine
Going to stay in bed all the time—so
(repeat)

# Baby Zodiac
## Birthstone & Symbol

### Aquarius
January 21 – February 18
Amethyst · Water Carrier

### Pisces
February 19 – March 20
Aquamarine · Fish

### Aries
March 21 – April 20
Diamond · Ram

### Taurus
April 21 – May 21
Emerald · Bull

### Gemini
May 22 – June 21
Pearl · Twins

### Cancer
June 22 – July 22
Ruby · Crab

# Baby Zodiac
## Birthstone & Symbol

### Leo
July 23 – August 23

Peridot · Lion

### Virgo
August 24 – September 22

Sapphire · Virgin

### Libra
September 23 – October 23

Opal · Scales

### Scorpio
October 24 – November 22

Topaz · Scorpion

### Sagittarius
November 23 – December 21

Turquoise · Archer

### Capricorn
December 22 – January 20

Garnet · Goat

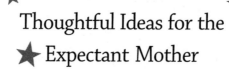

# Thoughtful Ideas for the Expectant Mother

Here's a list of some things that loved ones can do to make your pregnancy more enjoyable.

1. Tell her she's beautiful.

2. Take pictures of her, even if she doesn't want her picture taken. She'll appreciate it years later.

3. Compliment her.

4. Run her a bath. Use some nice fragrant bath salts.

5. Massage her body, especially where she needs it.

6. Go to doctor appointments with her.

7. Help out with the housework.

8. Send her cards and flowers.

9. Listen and talk to baby. Rub essential oils on stomach as you do this.

10. Plan outings. Do breakfast, lunch, dinner, or maybe just a lovely stroll along a beautiful park.

11. Buy her something special that you know she'll love— her favorite perfume, cute maternity outfit.

12. Cook for her.

13. Be supportive in every way possible.

# Things You Should Avoid Saying to the Expectant Mother

1. Never criticize her. She already feels like her body's changing in a million directions.
2. Never comment on her weight.
3. Never comment on how much weight she has gained.
4. Never even mention weight!

# All Children Are Gifts From God

## Children Are Blessings From God
PSALM 127:3-5

## God Carefully Creates Each Child
PSALM 139:13-16

## God Plans The Life Of Your Child
## Before He Or She Is Born
JEREMIAH 1:5

## Parents, Teach Your Children To Follow God
DEUTERONOMY 6:6-7

A is for "Adorable" you little bundle of joy!
So proud to be a parent of a baby girl or boy!

| | | |
|---|---|---|
| Aaliyah | Abebi | Abira |
| Aalvik | Abed | Ableson |
| Aaron | Abedin | Ablson |
| Aba | Abednego | Abner |
| Abacus | Abel | Abolute |
| Abasi | Abelia | Abra |
| Abba | Abena | Abraham |
| Abbett | Aberdeen | Abrahamson |
| Abbey | Aberion | Abram |
| Abbie | Aberle | Abrams |
| Abbigail | Aberly | Abran |
| Abbott | Abet | Abraxis |
| Abby | Abiah | Absala |
| Abdi | Abida | Absalom |
| Abdiel | Abiel | Absaraka |
| Abdol | Abigail | Absinthe |
| Abdul | Abigayle | Absolom |
| Abdulfatta | Abijah | Absolute |
| Abdulhadi | Abilene | Absynth |
| Abdullah | Abina | Abu |
| Abe | Abington | Abu-Najem |
| Abeba | Abir | Abu-Saleh |

| | | |
|---|---|---|
| Abu-Ulbeh | Active | Adella |
| Abuyan | Acton | Adellah |
| Abydiah | Acura | Adelle |
| Acacia | Ada | Adelpha |
| Acacio | Adael | Ademar |
| Acadia | Adagio | Aden |
| Acala | Adago | Adette |
| Acantha | Adah | Adiah |
| Acanthus | Adair | Adige |
| Acarai | Adalard | Adin |
| Acari | Adalberto | Adina |
| Acaria | Adalina | Adios |
| Acciura | Adaline | Adir |
| Acclaim | Adam | Adiva |
| Accord | Adamant | Adkin |
| Accura | Adamo | Adkins |
| Accurate | Adams | Adkinson |
| Ace | Adamson | Adlai |
| Achille | Adan | Adller |
| Achilles | Adara | Admire |
| Achir | Adaya | Adnan |
| Achord | Adaza | Adochas |
| Ackerman | Addi | Adolf |
| Ackerson | Addie | Adolfo |
| Ackia | Addison | Adolph |
| Acoka | Adela | Adolpho |
| Acola | Adelaide | Adolphus |
| Acosta | Adelard | Adom |
| Acre | Adelbert | Adon |
| Acree | Adele | Adoni |
| Act | Adelia | Adonis |
| Actin | Adelina | Adora |
| Action | Adeline | Adra |
| Activa | Adell | Adrain |

| | | |
|---|---|---|
| Adria | Afternoon | Aimee |
| Adrial | Afton | Aindria |
| Adrian | Agakhan | Aine |
| Adriana | Agate | Ainslee |
| Adriane | Agatha | Air |
| Adrianna | Agea | Aira |
| Adrianne | Ages | Airamus |
| Adriatic | Agnes | Airdria |
| Adriel | Agnew | Aisha |
| Adrien | Agree | Aisley |
| Adrienn | Aguon | Aisling |
| Adrienne | Agusta | Aja |
| Advance | Agustin | Ajax |
| Advent | Agustina | Ajudia |
| Adventure | Ahab | Akai |
| Advior | Ahem | Akbar |
| Advisor | Ahern | Akberet |
| Aed | Aherne | A'Kea |
| Aeddon | Ahmad | Akeem |
| Aedon | Ahmadi | Akela |
| Aelwyn | Ahmandi | Aken |
| Aengus | Ahmann | Akes |
| Aeola | Ahmed | Akia |
| Aeron | Ahren | Akiak |
| Aerton | Aida | Akil |
| Aerts | Aidan | Akilah |
| Aeschliman | Aideen | Akim |
| Aesir | Aiden | Akina |
| Affinity | Aiken | Akins |
| Afghan | Aileen | Akira |
| Afif | Ailey | Akmal |
| Afinity | Ailis | Akono |
| Africa | Ailsa | Akron |
| After | Aily | Aksel |

22

| | | |
|---|---|---|
| Akua | Albendo | Alecia |
| Al | Alberia | Aleen |
| Alabama | Albers | Alejandra |
| Alacyn | Albersa | Alejandrin |
| Alaia | Albert | Alejandro |
| Alain | Alberta | Alejo |
| Alaina | Albertha | Aleka |
| Alaine | Albertine | Aleksander |
| Alainya | Alberto | Aleksea |
| Alameda | Albin | Aleksia |
| Alamo | Albina | Alena |
| Alamosa | Albion | Alene |
| Alan | Albrecht | Alenia |
| Alana | Albreck | Alenington |
| Alane | Albria | Alesha |
| Alanis | Alburquerque | Alesia |
| Alanna | Alcala | Alessandra |
| Alar | Alcatraz | Alessia |
| Alaric | Alchemy | Aleta |
| Alasda | Alco | Alethea |
| Alasdae | Alcoa | Alex |
| Alasdai | Alcott | Alexa |
| Alaska | Alda | Alexander |
| Alastair | Alden | Alexandra |
| Alastar | Alder | Alexandre |
| Alayna | Alderman | Alexandrea |
| Alb | Alderson | Alexandria |
| Alba | Aldie | Alexandrina |
| Albane | Aldine | Alexandrine |
| Albania | Aldo | Alexandro |
| Albany | Aldrich | Alexandros |
| Albe | Aldridge | Alexia |
| Albedo | Aleah | Alexina |
| Albemari | Alec | Alexis |

| | | |
|---|---|---|
| Alexus | Alix | Allred |
| Alf | Aliya | Allura |
| Alfani | Aliyah | Allure |
| Alfonso | Aliz | Ally |
| Alfonzo | Aliza | Allyson |
| Alford | All | Allyssa |
| Alfred | Alla | Alma |
| Alfreda | Allah | Almallah |
| Alfredo | Al-Laham | Almeda |
| Alger | Allan | Al-Memar |
| Algeri | Allana | Almeta |
| Algeria | Allanie | Almetric |
| Algers | Allanna | Almira |
| Ali | Alldon | Almon |
| Alibi | Alledge | Almond |
| Alice | Allegra | Aloa |
| Alicia | Allen | Aloe |
| Alick | Allenbach | Aloesious |
| Alida | Allene | Aloha |
| Alika | Allerton | Alois |
| Alima | Allesio | Alolo |
| Alina | Allestad | Alondra |
| Alinka | Alley | Alondria |
| Alireza | Alleysen | Alongi |
| Alisa | Alleyton | Alonso |
| Alisha | Alli | Alonzo |
| Alishia | Alliance | Alor |
| Alisia | Allie | Aloysius |
| Alison | Alline | Alpha |
| Alissa | Allison | Alphonse |
| Aliv | Allon | Alphonso |
| Alive | Allot | Alps |
| Aliverti | Alloway | Al-Rashid |
| Alivo | Alloy | Al-Salman |

| | | |
|---|---|---|
| Alseth | Alyia | Ambrosia |
| Alston | Alyosha | Ambrosino |
| Alta | Alysa | Ambroz |
| Altair | Alyse | Amedeo |
| Al-Tamimi | Alysha | Amee |
| Altha | Alysia | Amelia |
| Althaia | Alyson | Amelie |
| Althauser | Alyssa | Amera |
| Althea | Alzeer | Amerah |
| Alther | Al-Zeer | Ameray |
| Altia | Amadeo | America |
| Alton | Amadeus | Americo |
| Aluin | Amado | Amerika |
| Alun | Amal | Amerson |
| Aluna | Amalia | Amery |
| Alunni | Amalya | Ames |
| Alura | Aman | Ami |
| Alva | Amanda | Amias |
| Alvah | Amando | Amie |
| Alvan | Amani | Amiee |
| Alvany | Amarae | Amiel |
| Alvarado | Amarosia | Amina |
| Alvarino | Amaya | Amir |
| Alvaro | Amaze | Amira |
| Alvena | Amazed | Amiri |
| Alvera | Amazen | Amity |
| Alverta | Amazing | Amjad |
| Alvie | Amber | Amma |
| Alvin | Ambera | Ammann |
| Alvina | Amberah | Amon |
| Alvis | Amberdawn | Amonann |
| Alxo | Ambra | Amos |
| Alyce | Ambroise | Amoz |
| Alycia | Ambrose | Amparo |

| | | |
|---|---|---|
| Amston | Andra | Angeline |
| Amundson | Andraya | Angelique |
| Amy | Andre | Angelita |
| An | André | Angelo |
| Ana | Andrea | Angeloff |
| Anabel | Andreas | Angie |
| Anabtawi | Andree | Angina |
| Anacon | Andreea | Angle |
| Anacreon | Andrei | Anglia |
| Anah | Andreini | Anglin |
| Anais | Andreotti | Angola |
| Analeese | Andres | Angrea |
| Analisa | Andress | Angstrom |
| Analogy | Andrew | Angus |
| Anastacio | Andrews | Anibal |
| Anastasia | Andrey | Anie |
| Anastazie | Andria | Anika |
| Anatola | Andries | Anina |
| Anatoli | Andromeda | Anissa |
| Anaximander | Andwynn | Anita |
| Ancheta | Andy | Anitra |
| Anchor | Aneira | Aniva |
| Anchorage | Anela | Anjanette |
| Ancich | Anette | Anjelica |
| Ancien | Angea | Anjelle |
| Ancona | Angehica | Ankara |
| Andale | Angel | Ankhnatun |
| Andalusia | Angela | Ann |
| Anders | Angelee | Anna |
| Andersen | Angeli | Annabel |
| Anderson | Angelia | Annabell |
| Andi | Angelica | Annabella |
| Andie | Angelika | Annabelle |
| Andor | Angelina | Annalisa |

Annamae
Annamarie
Anne
Anneka
Anneli
Annelid
Annemarie
Annerieka
Annetta
Annette
Annie
Annika
Anniki
Annis
Annisa
Annmarie
Annona
Anouilh
Anouk
Ansel
Anselm
Anselmo
Answer
Antaeus
Antarctica
Antawn
Anther
Anthia
Anthony
Antione
Antionette
Antoine
Antoinette
Anton

Antone
Antonella
Antonetta
Antonette
Antonia
Antonietta
Antonina
Antonio
Antony
Antwan
Antwon
Anwa
Anwar
Anya
Anyia
Anzelm
Aokay
Aoki
Apache
Aphrodite
Apocrypha
Apollo
Apollonia
Apolonia
Appel
Apple
Apricot
April
Aqua
Aquinas
Aquinnah
Ara
Arabella
Arabelle

Arabia
Arable
Araceli
Aragon
Arakelyan
Aram
Arango
Aranhia
Arani
Arawn
Arbon
Arbor
Arbra
Arbury
Arbus
Arc
Arcade
Arcadia
Arcadio
Arch
Archibald
Archibeque
Archie
Archimedes
Archipenko
Arco
Arctic
Ardell
Ardella
Arden
Ardesty
Ardis
Ardith
Ardon

| | | |
|---|---|---|
| Ardyce | Aristotle | Armen |
| Area | Arius | Armida |
| Arely | Ariza | Armijo |
| Areon | Arizona | Armon |
| Ares | Arjan | Armond |
| Aretha | Arjonet | Armor |
| Argan | Ark | Arms |
| Argentina | Arkadi | Armstrong |
| Argentine | Arkansas | Army |
| Argey | Arki | Arna |
| Argie | Arkin | Arnaldo |
| Argon | Arlane | Arnan |
| Argosy | Arlee | Arnbrister |
| Argus | Arleen | Arne |
| Ari | Arlen | Arneson |
| Aria | Arlene | Arney |
| Ariam | Arles | Arnica |
| Ariams | Arletta | Arnis |
| Ariana | Arlette | Arno |
| Arianna | Arley | Arnold |
| Aric | Arlice | Arnoldo |
| Arid | Arlie | Arnson |
| Arie | Arlin | Arnulfo |
| Ariel | Arline | Aron |
| Ariella | Arling | Aronson |
| Arielle | Arlington | Arouet |
| Aries | Arlis | Arquette |
| Arieta | Arlo | Array |
| Ario | Arly | Arretta |
| Arion | Arma | Arrid |
| Aris | Arman | Arrie |
| Arista | Armand | Arrington |
| Aristides | Armando | Arron |
| Aristophanes | Armani | Arrow |

Arseni
Arsenio
Arseno
Arshad
Art
Artas
Arteaga
Artemas
Artemi
Artemis
Arteria
Artesia
Artesian
Artezia
Arther
Arthur
Arthuro
Artic
Artie
Artis
Artisan
Artist
Artiste
Artistry
Arturo
Aruga
Arum
Aruna
Arusi
Arvai
Arvay
Arvel
Arvetta
Arvid

Arvil
Arvilla
Arvin
Arvo
Aryn
Asa
Asad
Asael
Asbach
Ascoli
Asercath
Ash
Asha
Ashanté
Ashanti
Ashbel
Ashby
Ashcroft
Ashe
Ashely
Asher
Ashes
Asheville
Ashland
Ashlee
Ashleigh
Ashley
Ashli
Ashlie
Ashlin
Ashlock
Ashly
Ashlyn
Ashlynn

Ashmore
Ashokan
Ashra
Ashton
Asia
Asifa
Asis
Askarian
Aske
Asklund
Aslan
Asmussen
Asner
Asoka
Asonant
Aspah
Aspen
Asriel
Assaf
Assanté
Assanti
Assaunta
Asseyev
Assisi
Assonance
Assunta
Asta
Aster
Astin
Astley
Aston
Astor
Astoria
Astra

| | | |
|---|---|---|
| Astrid | Aubert | Austen |
| Astro | Aubree | Austin |
| Asura | Aubrey | Australia |
| Ataila | Auburn | Austria |
| Atam | Audie | Austy |
| Atara | Audine | Austyn |
| Atasha | Audio | Auth |
| Atera | Audny | Auther |
| Atessa | Audra | Author |
| Athalia | Audran | Autio |
| Athena | Audras | Auto |
| Athens | Audree | Autonomy |
| Atherton | Audrey | Autrey |
| Athlete | Audric | Autry |
| Atilla | Augenstine | Autumn |
| Atkin | Augir | Auvil |
| Atkins | August | Ava |
| Atkinson | Augusta | Avalanche |
| Atlanta | Augustine | Avalon |
| Atlantic | Augustus | Avan |
| Atlantis | Aulene | Avanall |
| Atlantix | Aura | Avena |
| Atlas | Aurburn | Avenall |
| Atlatl | Aurea | Avenger |
| Atom | Aurelia | Avent |
| Aton | Aurelio | Avenue |
| Atticus | Auriga | Averi |
| Attila | Auron | Averill |
| Atwater | Aurora | Avery |
| Atwell | Aurore | Avey |
| Atwood | Auroroa | Avila |
| Atworth | Aurrora | Avinger |
| Atz | Ausband | Avis |
| Auberon | Aust | Aviv |

| | | |
|---|---|---|
| Avivah | Aydon | Azi |
| Avon | Ayeesha | Azibo |
| Avril | Ayers | Aziel |
| Awad | Ayla | Azim |
| Award | Ayne | Azimuth |
| Away | Ayo | Aziz |
| Awilda | Ayonna | Azizza |
| Axel | Ayres | Azmera |
| Axiom | Ayrton | Azrae |
| Axle | Az | Azriel |
| Axlund | Aza | Azsia |
| Axton | Azad | Aztec |
| Aya | Azai | Azteka |
| Ayana | Azalea | Azura |
| Ayanna | Azam | Azure |
| Ayasha | Azeca | Azuriah |
| Ayden | Azecca | |

31

B is for a little "Boy" sent from God above
A little soul he loaned to me, to care and give my love.

| | | |
|---|---|---|
| Ba | Bader | Bains |
| Baard | Baderdeen | Bainter |
| Baardson | Badger | Baio |
| Baba | Badu | Baird |
| Babar | Bae | Bairn |
| Babcock | Baene | Baker |
| Babery | Bagby | Bakke |
| Babson | Bagen | Bakotich |
| Babuca | Baghai | Bala |
| Baby | Bagley | Balachandran |
| Baca | Bagne | Balance |
| Bacall | Bahi | Balbas |
| Bacchus | Bahiradhan | Balboa |
| Bach | Bail | Bald |
| Bachman | Bailee | Baldauf |
| Back | Baileen | Baldemar |
| Backel | Baileigh | Baldridge |
| Backman | Bailen | Baldwin |
| Backus | Bailey | Bale |
| Bacon | Baily | Bales |
| Bacus | Bain | Baley |
| Baden | Bainbridge | Bali |

| | | |
|---|---|---|
| Balin | Barajas | Barnes |
| Ball | Barak | Barnett |
| Ballard | Barb | Barney |
| Ballentine | Barbados | Barnhart |
| Balmer | Barbara | Barnhill |
| Balogh | Barbary | Baroga |
| Balsam | Barber | Barolo |
| Balta | Barbera | Baron |
| Balthasar | Barberra | Barr |
| Balthrop | Barbi | Barrack |
| Baltic | Barbie | Barreck |
| Baltilmore | Barbra | Barren |
| Baltimore | Barcelona | Barrett |
| Balzac | Barcelone | Barrette |
| Bambi | Barclay | Barri |
| Bamboo | Barclift | Barrington |
| Banbri | Bard | Barrolli |
| Bancon | Bardiou | Barron |
| Band | Bardo | Barrow |
| Banda | Bardwell | Barrows |
| Bandy | Barea | Barry |
| Bangs | Bareé | Barsdale |
| Bank | Barge | Barsion |
| Banker | Barger | Barsness |
| Banks | Bari | Barsto |
| Banky | Bark | Barstow |
| Banner | Barker | Bart |
| Bannish | Barklow | Bartell |
| Bantam | Barley | Barth |
| Banter | Barlow | Barthelemy |
| Bantie | Barn | Bartholome |
| Bantry | Barnabas | Bartholomew |
| Baotu | Barnaby | Bartholomieu |
| Bara | Barnard | Bartley |

| | | |
|---|---|---|
| Bartman | Bauer | Beard |
| Barto | Baugh | Beardslee |
| Barton | Baun | Beardsley |
| Bartos | Bautista | Beat |
| Bartow | Baxter | Beata |
| Basha | Bay | Beatrice |
| Basham | Bayard | Beatriz |
| Bashon | Baydek | Beattie |
| Bashore | Bayer | Beatty |
| Basia | Bayha | Beaty |
| Basil | Baylee | Beau |
| Basila | Bayleigh | Beaudry |
| Basilio | Bayless | Beauf |
| Basilius | Bayonne | Beauford |
| Basin | Bayshore | Beaulah |
| Bass | Bayview | Beaulieu |
| Bastien | Baz | Beaumont |
| Bastin | Bazan | Beauregard |
| Bat | Baze | Beauty |
| Batch | Bazel | Beauvier |
| Batcheldor | Bazil | Beaver |
| Batchelor | Bea | Bebe |
| Bateman | Beacan | Beca |
| Bates | Beach | Becarra |
| Bath | Beacham | Becca |
| Bathsheba | Beacher | Becci |
| Batik | Beacon | Becerra |
| Baton | Beah | Becher |
| Batta | Beaird | Beck |
| Batterton | Beal | Becka |
| Batties | Beals | Becke |
| Battin | Beam | Becken |
| Battiste | Beamer | Becker |
| Bauch | Bean | Beckley |

Beckman
Becky
Beddo
Bede
Beder
Bedi
Bedrock
Bee
Beebe
Beebee
Beech
Beeman
Beemer
Begin
Beierle
Beige
Bekin
Bela
Belcher
Belden
Belding
Beldon
Belen
Belfair
Belfry
Belgian
Belgin
Belia
Belin
Belinda
Bell
Bella
Bellamy
Belle

Beller
Bellevue
Bellinger
Belmont
Belqies
Belton
Belva
Bely
Bemuse
Ben
Bena
Benaca
Benaiah
Benaigh
Bend
Bendix
Bendzak
Beneba
Beneca
Benedict
Benenati
Benham
Benicio
Benisha
Benita
Benito
Benizia
Benjamen
Benjamin
Benjamina
Benner
Bennett
Bennette
Bennie

Bennion
Benno
Benny
Benoît
Benoni
Bensinger
Benson
Bentley
Benton
Bentow
Bentsen
Benz
Beranek
Berea
Bereded
Berek
Beren
Berenda
Berends
Berenice
Berens
Berensten
Beret
Beretta
Berezin
Berg
Bergamot
Bergdolt
Berge
Bergeman
Bergen
Berger
Bergerac
Bergh

| | | |
|---|---|---|
| Bergman | Berrian | Betti |
| Bergquam | Berry | Bettie |
| Bergren | Bert | Bettina |
| Bergstrom | Berta | Betty |
| Berinelli | Berth | Bettye |
| Berintsen | Bertha | Beulah |
| Berk | Berthy | Bevan |
| Berkan | Berti | Beverley |
| Berkeley | Bertie | Beverly |
| Berken | Bertin | Bevin |
| Berker | Bertl | Bevington |
| Berkey | Bertle | Bex |
| Berkley | Berton | Bexlen |
| Berlin | Bertram | Beyer |
| Berm | Bertrand | Beyersdorf |
| Bermise | Bertsch | Beyonca |
| Bermuda | Bertucci | Beyonce |
| Bermudez | Beryl | Beyoncé |
| Bern | Beseda | Beyond |
| Bernadette | Beshaler | Beyouce |
| Bernadine | Bess | Beyouncá |
| Bernard | Bessie | BeYounce |
| Bernardine | Best | Bezel |
| Bernardo | Beste | Bezelle |
| Berne | Bet | Bhalla |
| Berneice | Beth | Bharil |
| Berner | Bethan | Bhutan |
| Bernhard | Bethany | Bi |
| Bernhardt | Bethel | Biaggio |
| Bernice | Betheny | Biagio |
| Bernie | Bethia | Bianca |
| Berniece | Betsi | Bianchi |
| Bernita | Betsy | Bianka |
| Berretta | Bette | Biasotti |

36

| | | |
|---|---|---|
| Bice | Binker | Blade |
| Bich | Binns | Bladen |
| Bickle | Binta | Blades |
| Biddle | Biranma | Blaine |
| Bidelia | Birch | Blair |
| Bienvenido | Bircher | Blaise |
| Bierce | Bird | Blake |
| Bierschbach | Birdie | Blakely |
| Bigelow | Birdsall | Blakley |
| Biggs | Biren | Blalock |
| Bigler | Birget | Blanca |
| Bijan | Birkett | Blanch |
| Bijou | Birney | Blanchard |
| Bike | Birr | Blanche |
| Biker | Birrenkott | Blanco |
| Bilhedidd | Birtle | Bland |
| Bill | Biscayne | Blanda |
| Billie | Bischoff | Blanden |
| Billing | Bishop | Blane |
| Billings | Bismarck | Blaney |
| Billingsley | Bitar | Blank |
| Billion | Bithia | Blanken |
| Billy | Bitney | Blanton |
| Billy Bob | Bittick | Blass |
| Billye | Bitton | Blast |
| Bilo | Bjordahl | Blau |
| Biloxi | Bjork | Blayn |
| Bina | Bjorn | Blayney |
| Binaca | Black | Blaze |
| Bind | Blacke | Blazon |
| Binder | Blackie | Bleecker |
| Bing | Blackly | Blegen |
| Binh | Blacksmith | Blend |
| Bink | Blacky | Blende |

| | | |
|---|---|---|
| Blennie | Bobina | Bone |
| Bless | Boc | Bongo |
| Blevins | Bode | Bonita |
| Blink | Bodey | Bonn |
| Blinker | Bodin | Bonner |
| Blinkin | Bodine | Bonnie |
| Block | Boe | Bonnye |
| Blomberg | Boettcher | Bono |
| Blomquist | Boey | Bonwell |
| Bloom | Bogachiel | Boo |
| Bloomer | Bogart | Book |
| Blossom | Bogata | Booker |
| Blue | Boggi | Books |
| Bluff | Bogota | Boone |
| Blum | Bogue | Booth |
| Blune | Boheme | Borchers |
| Blush | Bohm | Borden |
| Blythe | Bohnet | Border |
| Bo | Boibeal | Borek |
| Boat | Bois | Boris |
| Boatright | Boise | Borland |
| Boaye | Bolam | Borley |
| Boaz | Bolden | Born |
| Bob | Boldt | Borne |
| Boba | Bolduc | Borsch |
| Bobbert | Bolin | Bortle |
| Bobbette | Bolivar | Borts |
| Bobbi | Bolivia | Borvo |
| Bobbie | Bolley | Boston |
| Bobby | Bolman | Bosworth |
| Bobettee | Bolton | Boucher |
| Bobi | Bolyard | Bouk |
| Bobia | Bon Jovi | Boulder |
| Bobie | Bond | Bouler |

| | | |
|---|---|---|
| Boultinghouse | Boysen | Brakar |
| Bounce | Boz | Brake |
| Bouncé | Bozanich | Braksma |
| Bounchoeu | Bozidar | Bralen |
| Boundary | Brac | Braley |
| Bounder | Brace | Bralith |
| Bourbon | Brach | Bramen |
| Bourgault | Brack | Bramley |
| Bourne | Bracken | Brampton |
| Boutilier | Brad | Bramsen |
| Bouvier | Bradan | Brana |
| Bovina | Braddoc | Branch |
| Bow | Braddock | Brand |
| Bowden | Braden | Brandan |
| Bowdon | Bradentine | Brandee |
| Bowen | Bradenton | Brandell |
| Bower | Bradford | Branden |
| Bowers | Brading | Brandenburg |
| Bowie | Bradington | Brandi |
| Bowker | Bradlee | Brandie |
| Bowler | Bradley | Brandland |
| Bowles | Bradly | Brandn |
| Bowling | Bradner | Brandon |
| Bowman | Brado | Brandt |
| Bown | Bradshaw | Brandy |
| Box | Bradten | Brandyn |
| Boy | Bradton | Branef |
| Boyce | Brady | Branko |
| Boyd | Braese | Brannif |
| Boyde | Braga | Brannock |
| Boydton | Bragdon | Brannon |
| Boyer | Bragnwynne | Branquin |
| Boyle | Braise | Branson |
| Boynton | Braison | Bransyn |

| | | |
|---|---|---|
| Brant | Breaz | Brennen |
| Brantford | Breaza | Brent |
| Branwyn | Breccan | Brenton |
| Brasch | Breck | Breonna |
| Brascher | Breckan | Brescia |
| Brass | Brecken | Bret |
| Braten | Breckenridge | Breton |
| Bratlee | Breckin | Brett |
| Bratt | Breckinridge | Bretthauer |
| Bratton | Brecklan | Brew |
| Brauer | Breckly | Brewer |
| Brauhn | Bree | Brewster |
| Brauk | Breeanna | Breyen |
| Braun | Breese | Breze |
| Brave | Breeson | Bria |
| Bravo | Breeze | Brian |
| Brawley | Breezee | Briana |
| Braxmeyer | Breezie | Brianna |
| Braxton | Breezy | Brianne |
| Bray | Breiah | Briar |
| Brayan | Breian | Brice |
| Brayden | Breien | Bricheux |
| Braydon | Breland | Brick |
| Braymer | Bremen | Brickly |
| Brazil | Bremjit | Brickman |
| Brazzel | Bremmer | Bridge |
| Bre | Bremner | Bridgeport |
| Brea | Brenda | Bridger |
| Breah | Brendan | Bridges |
| Breana | Brenden | Bridget |
| Breann | Brendon | Bridgett |
| Breanna | Brenna | Bridgette |
| Breanne | Brennan | Bridie |
| Breaux | Brenneis | Bridle |

| | | |
|---|---|---|
| Brie | Brisbe | Brockston |
| Briele | Brisboise | Brockton |
| Brielle | Briscoe | Brocton |
| Brien | Brishen | Brodeck |
| Brier | Brissae | Broden |
| Brieze | Bristol | Broderick |
| Brigette | Bristow | Broderius |
| Briggs | Brit | Brodeur |
| Brigham | Britain | Brodin |
| Bright | Britania | Brody |
| Brighten | Britany | Broen |
| Brightman | British | Brogan |
| Brighton | Britney | Broke |
| Brigitte | Britni | Broken |
| Briglia | Britt | Brokke |
| Briklin | Britta | Brokken |
| Brill | Brittani | Bron |
| Brillian | Brittania | Bronco |
| Brilliant | Brittanie | Brone |
| Brilliantine | Brittany | Bronham |
| Brillig | Brittland | Bronson |
| Brillion | Brittle | Bronte |
| Brilon | Brittnacy | Bronwynne |
| Brim | Brittney | Bronze |
| Bring | Brittni | Brook |
| Brings | Brittny | Brookbank |
| Brink | Britton | Brooke |
| Brinkin | Britty | Brooker |
| Brinkley | Brix | Brooklon |
| Brinks | Briyana | Brooklyn |
| Brinson | Brizendine | Brooklynne |
| Brion | Broadsword | Brooks |
| Bris | Broadway | Brophy |
| Brisbane | Brock | Brose |

| | | |
|---|---|---|
| Brosio | Bryce | Bump |
| Bross | Brycen | Bunch |
| Broughton | Brychan | Bundy |
| Brouillard | Bryn | Bunkie |
| Brow | Bryon | Buoy |
| Brown | Bryson | Burbank |
| Browning | Buare | Burbery |
| Browse | Bubble | Burchak |
| Broxton | Bubbles | Burdette |
| Brozovich | Buck | Burdick |
| Bruce | Buckenmeyer | Burdock |
| Bruceton | Buckle | Burford |
| Bruhn | Buckled | Burgandie |
| Bruin | Bucklette | Burgess |
| Bruit | Buckley | Burglind |
| Brumfield | Buckner | Burgundy |
| Brummitt | Bud | Burke |
| Brun | Buddy | Burkey |
| Bruner | Budell | Burkholder |
| Brunette | Budley | Burl |
| Brunhirl | Bueckers | Burley |
| Brunilda | Buehler | Burlingame |
| Bruno | Buehn | Burlington |
| Brunson | Buffie | Burma |
| Brush | Buffy | Burmese |
| Bruskiewicz | Buford | Burmus |
| Brusser | Bugatti | Burn |
| Brut | Bui | Burnell |
| Brx | Bukowski | Burnett |
| Bryan | Bulah | Burney |
| Bryana | Bullamore | Burnham |
| Bryanna | Bullard | Burnice |
| Bryanne | Bulto | Burnie |
| Bryant | Bulzomi | Burns |

Burnside
Burnt
Burr
Burri
Burroughs
Burrus
Burt
Burton
Burundi
Busby

Busch
Busche
Bush
Bushnaq
Bushnell
Busi
Buster
Butch
Butler
Butte

Butterfield
Butterfly
Butters
Butterworth
By
Byrd
Byrne
Byrnn
Byron

C is for "Caring" throughout all your years.
I'll always be here to dry all your tears.

| | | |
|---|---|---|
| Cab | Cadillac | Calais |
| Caballero | Cadiz | Calamity |
| Cabana | Cadoc | Calander |
| Cabaret | Caesar | Calandra |
| Cabasco | Cafe | Calder |
| Cabe | Caffey | Caldera |
| Cabell | Cage | Calderon |
| Cabery | Cagery | Caldwell |
| Cabiao | Cahill | Cale |
| Cable | Cai | Caleb |
| Cabot | Cailen | Caledonia |
| Cabrera | Cain | Caleigh |
| Cache | Cairn | Calek |
| Cacher | Cairnes | Calen |
| Cachet | Cairo | Calendar |
| Cactus | Cait | Calera |
| Cadagan | Caitlin | Caley |
| Cadby | Caitlyn | Calgary |
| Caddell | Cake | Calhoun |
| Cade | Cal | Cali |
| Caden | Cala | Calian |
| Cades | Calabria | Calico |

| | | |
|---|---|---|
| California | Camelia | Candence |
| Calihan | Camella | Candi |
| Calinda | Camen | Candice |
| Calion | Cameo | Candido |
| Calissa | Camera | Candis |
| Calista | Camerer | Candle |
| Caliva | Cameron | Candy |
| Calkins | Cameroon | Cane |
| Calla | Camerton | Canfield |
| Callahan | Camila | Cannizzaro |
| Callais | Camilla | Cannon |
| Callao | Camille | Canoe |
| Callar | Camisha | Canola |
| Callen | Cam-Le | Canon |
| Callie | Cammer | Canter |
| Callista | Camp | Canterbury |
| Callow | Campanelli | Canticle |
| Callum | Campbell | Cantil |
| Calro | Campbellton | Canto |
| Calrod | Campden | Canton |
| Calsy | Camper | Cantrell |
| Calundann | Camrin | Cantu |
| Calvary | Camron | Canyon |
| Calvin | Camus | Cap |
| Calypso | Camy | Capacity |
| Camacho | Canaan | Cape |
| Camano | Canaba | Capella |
| Camaro | Canada | Capps |
| Camas | Canal | Capri |
| Camay | Canby | Caprice |
| Cambell | Candace | Car |
| Cambridge | Candar | Cara |
| Camden | Candelario | Caralson |
| Camel | Candell | Caraway |

45

| | | |
|---|---|---|
| Carbajal | Carlos | Carrell |
| Card | Carlota | Carrera |
| Carden | Carlotta | Carri |
| Carder | Carlson | Carriage |
| Cardoni | Carlton | Carrie |
| Care | Carly | Carrigan |
| Career | Carlyle | Carrissa |
| Carelly | Carma | Carrol |
| Caren | Carmel | Carroll |
| Carera | Carmela | Carrolly |
| Carerra | Carmelita | Carron |
| Carew | Carmella | Carrot |
| Carey | Carmelo | Carruth |
| Cari | Carmen | Carry |
| Caria | Carmine | Carson |
| Carie | Carmona | Carst |
| Cariker | Carnage | Carsten |
| Carina | Carne | Carta |
| Caring | Carnegie | Cartahena |
| Carisa | Carnell | Carte |
| Carissa | Carnes | Cartegena |
| Cariza | Carney | Carter |
| Carl | Caro | Cartier |
| Carla | Carol | Cartner |
| Carlee | Carola | Cartwright |
| Carlene | Carole | Caruso |
| Carler | Carolina | Carva |
| Carleton | Caroline | Carvalho |
| Carley | Carolyn | Carvall |
| Carli | Carolynn | Carvell |
| Carlie | Carpenter | Carver |
| Carlile | Carpul | Cary |
| Carlin | Carr | Caryl |
| Carlo | Carrea | Caryn |

| | | |
|---|---|---|
| Cas | Catalina | Causland |
| Casa | Catania | Cavanagh |
| Casandra | Catarina | Cavanaugh |
| Cascade | Cate | Cave |
| Case | Cater | Caver |
| Casey | Caterian | Caviar |
| Cash | Caterina | Cawthon |
| Casi | Cates | Cayden |
| Casiano | Catharine | Cayene |
| Casie | Catherine | Cayenne |
| Casimer | Cathie | Cayla |
| Casimir | Cathleen | Cayley |
| Casino | Cathrine | Cayman |
| Casis | Cathryn | Caz |
| Caskey | Cathy | Cazin |
| Casleg | Catia | Cazt |
| Cason | Catie | Cealer |
| Casper | Catina | Ceara |
| Caspian | Cation | Cebell |
| Cass | Catlin | Cebo |
| Cassandra | Cato | Cebriak |
| Cassidy | Caton | Cecelia |
| Cassie | Catrina | Cecil |
| Cassini | Catriona | Cecile |
| Cast | Cats | Cecilia |
| Castillo | Catthi | Cecilio |
| Castle | Cattin | Cecily |
| Castler | Caty | Cedar |
| Castor | Catz | Cedell |
| Castro | Caufman | Cedric |
| Casual | Cauley | Cedrick |
| Caswell | Caulk | Ceil |
| Cat | Caullen | Ceileen |
| Cata | Cause | Ceiliene |

| | | |
|---|---|---|
| Ceiling | Cerus | Chaise |
| Ceilion | Cervine | Cha'la |
| Ceirra | Cesar | Chalisa |
| Celedonia | Cesaro | Chalk |
| Celena | Cessna | Challenge |
| Celene | C'Est | Chamber |
| Celeriac | Cetacia | Chamberlain |
| Celery | Cetacian | Chambers |
| Celeste | Cetera | Chamblin |
| Celestine | Cetus | Champ |
| Celestino | Ceva | Champagne |
| Celia | Ceylon | Champagnelle |
| Celilo | Cezar | Champie |
| Celina | Chad | Champion |
| Celine | Chadd | Chan |
| Celta | Chadden | Chana |
| Celvia | Chadderton | Chance |
| Cenaro | Chaddon | Chancellor |
| Cendell | Chaden | Chanda |
| Centar | Chadon | Chandell |
| Centaur | Chadra | Chandler |
| Centauri | Chadrick | Chandra |
| Centennial | Chadron | Chanel |
| Center | Chadvon | Chanelle |
| Central | Chadwick | Chaney |
| Centralia | Chaffee | Chang |
| Century | Chaffey | Changchien |
| Cerf | Chagrin | Change |
| Cerise | Chai | Channa |
| Cernick | Chaika | Channel |
| Cerone | Chaim | Channell |
| Cerril | Chain | Channing |
| Cerrillo | Chainey | Chantal |
| Certify | Chair | Chante |

Chantel
Chantelle
Chanti
Chantilly
Chantrelle
Chapin
Chapman
Chappell
Char
Charaton
Charbonneau
Chardonnay
Chare
Chargualaf
Charis
Charissa
Charisse
Chariton
Charity
Charla
Charlain
Charlebois
Charlene
Charles
Charleston
Charley
Charlie
Charline
Charlise
Charliz
Charlize
Charlotte
Charlsey
Charlsie

Charlton
Charlyize
Charm
Charma
Charmaine
Charmian
Charms
Charna
Charo
Charon
Charpilloz
Charryn
Chart
Charter
Chartic
Chas
Chase
Chasen
Chaser
Chasey
Chasez
Chason
Chassell
Chastity
Chatham
Chatterton
Chatwin
Chau
Chauncey
Chaussee
Chaves
Chavez
Chavis
Chaya

Chayce
Chaz
Chazmir
Chazon
Chazy
Chazz
Ché
Chea
Cheaha
Cheatham
Chechowitz
Check
Checker
Cheech
Cheeny
Chehalis
Cheila
Chek
Chekhov
Chel
Chela
Chelan
Cheledinas
Chelly
Chelone
Chelsea
Chelsey
Chelsi
Chelsie
Chelyan
Chen
Chena
Cheney
Chenik

| | | |
|---|---|---|
| Chenna | Chevis | Chisholm |
| Chepel | Chevonne | Chiusi |
| Cher | Chevron | Chloe |
| Cherfe | Chevy | Cho |
| Cheri | Cheyanne | Choi |
| Cherice | Cheyenne | Choice |
| Cherie | Chez | Choose |
| Cheriel | Chi | Chopp |
| Cherile | Chia | Chord |
| Cherilee | Chiara | Chorus |
| Cherilyn | Chiata | Chosen |
| Cherise | Chicago | Chris |
| Cherish | Chick | Chrissy |
| Cherokee | Chicka | Christ |
| Cherry | Chico | Christa |
| Cherwien | Chief | Christal |
| Cheryl | Chieppa | Christeen |
| Cheryle | Chi-Fai | Christel |
| Cheryll | Child | Christen |
| Chesi | Childer | Christene |
| Chesley | Childs | Christensen |
| Chesney | Chili | Christenson |
| Chess | Chill | Christi |
| Chesstine | Chillan | Christian |
| Chessy | Chillian | Christiana |
| Chester | Chimera | Christiansen |
| Chestnut | Chin | Christianson |
| Chet | China | Christie |
| Cheung | Chinasia | Christin |
| Chevak | Ching | Christina |
| Chevas | Chinook | Christine |
| Cheven | Chip | Christmas |
| Chevery | Chira | Christo |
| Cheves | Chisel | Christobal |

| | | |
|---|---|---|
| Christoffer | Cindel | Claton |
| Christon | Cindell | Claud |
| Christop | Cinder | Claude |
| Christoper | Cindi | Claudette |
| Christopher | Cindy | Claudia |
| Christophersen | Cinnamon | Claudie |
| Christy | Cipher | Claudine |
| Chrity | Circle | Claudio |
| Chrome | Cirrus | Clausen |
| Chrysalis | Cisco | Clauson |
| Chrystal | Cissna | Claxon |
| Chu | Cita | Clay |
| Chuck | Citare | Claybo |
| Chum | City | Clayborn |
| Chumley | Civic | Claybrook |
| Chun | Civil | Claycamp |
| Church | Clafin | Clayson |
| Churchill | Clair | Clayton |
| Churney | Claire | Clayville |
| Chute | Clancy | Claywell |
| Cian | Clandan | Clea |
| Ciar | Clara | Cleadom |
| Ciara | Clarabelle | Clear |
| Ciccone | Clarance | Clearlake |
| Cicero | Clare | Clearly |
| Cichowski | Clarence | Cleatus |
| Ciera | Claribel | Cleaver |
| Cieri | Clarice | Clell |
| Cierra | Clarine | Clem |
| Cihon | Clarissa | Cleman |
| Cilia | Clark | Clemen |
| Cimarron | Clarke | Clemency |
| Cincinatti | Clarkson | Clemens |
| Cinda | Class | Clemensen |

| | | |
|---|---|---|
| Clement | Clocke | Code |
| Clementina | Cloe | Codey |
| Clementine | Cloey | Codie |
| Clements | Close | Cody |
| Clemmie | Closer | Coe |
| Clemons | Clostio | Coelleen |
| Cleo | Cloud | Coffland |
| Cleon | Cloudy | Coffman |
| Cleopatra | Clouse | Cognac |
| Cleora | Clove | Cohen |
| Cleta | Cloven | Cohn |
| Cletis | Clover | Coin |
| Cletus | Clovis | Coke |
| Cleve | Cloyd | Cokie |
| Cleveland | Club | Cola |
| Clevenger | Clyde | Colbal |
| Clever | Coal | Colburn |
| Clibborn | Coast | Colby |
| Cliff | Coastal | Cold |
| Clifford | Coat | Colden |
| Clift | Coates | Cole |
| Clifton | Coats | Coleen |
| Clima | Cobalt | Coleman |
| Climale | Cobb | Colete |
| Climate | Cobe | Coletta |
| Climb | Coben | Colette |
| Climentine | Cobra | Coley |
| Cline | Coburg | Colgate |
| Clint | Coby | Colier |
| Clinton | Coca | Colin |
| Cliv | Cochise | Colleague |
| Clive | Cochran | Colleen |
| Clo | Coco | College |
| Clock | Cocoa | Collen |

| | | |
|---|---|---|
| Collette | Company | Conra |
| Collie | Compass | Conrad |
| Collier | Compassion | Conroy |
| Collin | Compet | Cons |
| Collins | Compton | Consonance |
| Collio | Comstock | Consonant |
| Colm | Conall | Consort |
| Cologne | Conan | Constance |
| Colombia | Concetta | Constantin |
| Colombo | Conconully | Consuela |
| Color | Concord | Consuelo |
| Colorado | Conde | Contact |
| Colson | Condee | Contend |
| Colt | Condo | Content |
| Colten | Condor | Conway |
| Colter | Condotta | Conyers |
| Colton | Cong | Coo |
| Colum | Congo | Cook |
| Columbia | Conk | Cooke |
| Columbus | Conklin | Cookey |
| Colver | Conley | Cookie |
| Colwyn | Conn | Cooler |
| Coman | Connecticut | Cooley |
| Comanche | Connee | Coolidge |
| Combs | Connell | Coop |
| Comer | Connelley | Cooper |
| Comet | Conner | Coor |
| Comfort | Connery | Coors |
| Comfrey | Connett | Coos |
| Comfy | Conney | Cope |
| Commadore | Connie | Copley |
| Comment | Connor | Copper |
| Commit | Connya | Cor |
| Como | Conor | Cora |

53

| | | |
|---|---|---|
| Coral | Cornelius | Coulon |
| Coralissa | Cornell | Coulter |
| Coralson | Corona | Counsel |
| Corbain | Corpus | Counselor |
| Corbet | Corral | Count |
| Corbett | Correa | Countess |
| Corbin | Correlle | Country |
| Corbit | Corrie | County |
| Corcoran | Corrina | Court |
| Cord | Corrine | Courtenea |
| Cordelia | Corrosia | Courtesy |
| Cordell | Cort | Courtland |
| Cordia | Cortas | Courtnay |
| Cordie | Cortez | Courtney |
| Cordova | Cortney | Courtois |
| Corelly | Cortnie | Cousanne |
| Corene | Cortnik | Cousin |
| Corey | Corvette | Cousins |
| Corgatelli | Cory | Couture |
| Cori | Cosecant | Couver |
| Corianne | Cosem | Cove |
| Corie | Cosine | Covell |
| Corina | Cosmic | Covet |
| Corine | Cosmo | Covington |
| Corinna | Cosmos | Cowan |
| Corinne | Costas | Cowboy |
| Corkett | Cota | Cowell |
| Corlett | Cote | Cowger |
| Corliss | Cotten | Cox |
| Cormick | Cotton | Coy |
| Corn | Coty | Coyle |
| Corneille | Couch | Cozette |
| Cornelia | Coug | Cozian |
| Cornelis | Cougar | Cozley |

| | | |
|---|---|---|
| Crag | Crest | Croix |
| Crager | Crestent | Crompton |
| Craggs | Cresto | Cromwell |
| Craig | Creston | Cronenwett |
| Craik | Cretu | Cronk |
| Crain | Crevice | Crookshank |
| Cramer | Crevis | Crosby |
| Crandal | Creviston | Cross |
| Crane | Crew | Crosser |
| Cranley | Crickmer | Crossing |
| Cranston | Crigler | Crossley |
| Crass | Crimea | Croston |
| Crate | Crimson | Crouse |
| Crater | Cris | Crow |
| Crawford | Crisha | Crowel |
| Crayton | Crisman | Crowell |
| Creak | Crispin | Crown |
| Cream | Crissy | Croz |
| Create | Crist | Crozley |
| Credita | Crista | Cruger |
| Cree | Cristal | Cruise |
| Creed | Cristian | Crum |
| Creede | Cristin | Crumb |
| Creedence | Cristina | Crumbley |
| Creek | Cristobal | Crump |
| Creevan | Cristopher | Crusade |
| Crelli | Cristy | Crush |
| Crenshaw | Criswell | Cruz |
| Creola | Criteria | Cruze |
| Crerar | Criterion | Crystal |
| Crescent | Crizan | Cuba |
| Cresent | Crockett | Cuc |
| Cressa | Croft | Cuff |
| Cressida | Crofton | Cuise |

Cullen
Culp
Culture
Culver
Cummings
Cummins
Cunningham
Cupid
Curent
Cureton
Curiosity
Curlew
Curran
Currant
Current
Curry
Curt
Curtis

Curtiss
Curve
Cushman
Cusic
Custom
Cutie
Cutiepie
Cutler
Cutter
Cuyler
Cuzick
Cuzy
Cyan
Cycle
Cydney
Cyford
Cylee
Cyler

Cymbal
Cymon
Cynder
Cyndi
Cyndie
Cyndy
Cynthia
Cypher
Cypress
Cyprus
Cyra
Cyrano
Cyrena
Cyress
Cyril
Cyrus
Czarina

D is for "Daddy," who keeps you safe and warm,
while providing shelter from life's many storms.

| | | |
|---|---|---|
| Da Ná | Dailey | Dalle |
| Daalmeyer | Daily | Dalles |
| Dabbs | Dainty | Dallin |
| Dabney | Daira | Dally |
| Dacey | Daire | Dalmeny |
| Dacia | Dairus | Dalsten |
| Dade | Daisy | Dalt |
| Dado | Dakar | Dalton |
| Dadye | Daker | Daltrey |
| Dael | Dakota | Daltry |
| Daffodil | Dakotah | Daly |
| Dafney | Dalai | Dalya |
| Dag | Dalanee | Dalyn |
| Dagmar | Dale | Damarcus |
| Dagny | Daleane | Damario |
| Dahlgren | Dalene | Damaris |
| Dahlia | Daley | Damascus |
| Dahlke | Dalfrey | Damden |
| Dahna | Dalfus | Dame |
| Dahomey | Dalia | Damean |
| Dai | Dalilia | Dameetre |
| Daida | Dallas | Damek |

| | | |
|---|---|---|
| Dameon | Danika | Darcy |
| Damian | Danil | Dare |
| Damien | Danile | Darell |
| Damion | Danilowicz | Daren |
| Damitio | Danisha | Daresa |
| Damon | Danissa | Darhl |
| Damron | Danita | Dari |
| Dan | Danitta | Daria |
| Dana | Danna | Darian |
| Danaace | Danne | Darien |
| Danar | Danné | Darilyn |
| Danaus | Danner | Darin |
| Dance | Dannette | Daring |
| Dancer | Dannie | Dario |
| Dandre | Danninger | Darion |
| Dane | Danny | Darissa |
| Dané | Danon | Darius |
| Daneen | Dansal | Dark |
| Danelle | Danson | Darla |
| Danessa | Dante | Darleen |
| Danette | Dantzler | Darlene |
| Danforth | Danu | Darline |
| Dangelo | Danyel | Darling |
| Danger | Danyelle | Darlington |
| Danhya | Daphne | Darma |
| Dani | Daquan | Darneille |
| Dania | Dar | Darnell |
| Danial | Dara | Darnett |
| Danica | Darbie | Darnick |
| Daniel | Darby | Daroga |
| Daniela | Darce | Darold |
| Daniella | Darcel | Daron |
| Danielle | Darci | Darrah |
| Daniels | Darcie | Darrel |

| | | |
|---|---|---|
| Darrell | David | Deacon |
| Darren | Davidson | Deal |
| Darrian | Davies | Dealer |
| Darrick | Davin | Dean |
| Darrien | Davina | Deana |
| Darrin | Davion | Deandra |
| Darrion | Davis | Deandre |
| Darrius | Davison | Deane |
| Darron | Davon | Deangelique |
| Darry | Davonte | Deangelo |
| Darryl | Davos | Deanie |
| Dart | Davy | Deann |
| Darwhi | Daw | Deanna |
| Darwin | Dawber | Deanne |
| Darwish | Dawk | Dearda |
| Darwood | Dawn | Deardorf |
| Daryelle | Dawna | Deardra |
| Daryl | Dawndi | Deats |
| Daryle | Daws | Deb |
| Dash | Dawson | Debbie |
| Dashawn | Dax | Debby |
| Dashiel | Daxz | Debi |
| Dassel | Day | Debil |
| Data | Dayen | Debolt |
| Date | Dayle | Debora |
| Datil | Daylee | Deborah |
| Datum | Daymon | Debord |
| Daubert | Daymond | Debra |
| Daugherty | Dayn | Debrina |
| Dauphine | Dayna | Decade |
| Daura | Dayton | Decaro |
| Davari | Daytona | Decarufel |
| Dave | De | Decatur |
| Davey | De Neá | Deccio |

59

| | | |
|---|---|---|
| December | Deidra | Delores |
| Decino | Deidre | Delori |
| Deck | Deidrich | Deloris |
| Decker | Deion | Delpha |
| Deckert | Deirdre | Delphia |
| Declan | Deitra | Delphine |
| Declare | Deity | Delta |
| Dedalia | Deja | Delton |
| Dedinsky | Dejon | Delvin |
| Dedra | Dejong | Delwar |
| Dedric | Dejuan | Delzer |
| Dedrick | Del | Demarco |
| Dee | Delacruz | Demarcus |
| Deea | Delaney | Demario |
| Deeandra | Delange | Demaris |
| Deede | Delaware | Demas |
| Deedee | Delbert | Demery |
| Deedra | Deleon | Demestre |
| Deek | Delfina | Demetra |
| Deemer | Delgado | Demetri |
| Deemo | Delhi | Demetria |
| Deemona | Delia | Demetris |
| Deena | Delicia | Demetrius |
| Deep | Delilah | Demi |
| Deer | Delio | Demitri |
| Deere | Delisa | Demo |
| Deerlin | Dell | Demond |
| Deeter | Della | Demory |
| Deforest | Delle | Demott |
| Defries | Delli | Dempsey |
| Degenhart | Dellinger | Dena |
| Degolier | Delma | Denae |
| Degroat | Delmar | Denai |
| Deichl | Delmer | Denali |

| | | |
|---|---|---|
| Denbo | Dereck | Dessolene |
| Dene | Derek | Destin |
| Dené | Deric | Destinee |
| Denee | Derick | Destiney |
| Deneen | Derik | Destini |
| Denes | Dermott | Destiny |
| Deni | Deron | Destry |
| Denice | Derrell | Deter |
| Denis | Derrick | Dethlefs |
| Denise | Derway | Detroit |
| Denisse | Derwin | Detton |
| Denley | Deschane | Deuce |
| Denmark | Deschutes | Deundre |
| Denn | Desdemona | Devan |
| Dennard | Dereá | Devante |
| Dennie | Deseret | Devaul |
| Denning | Desert | Devel |
| Dennis | Deshaun | Deven |
| Denny | Deshawn | Deverall |
| Dens | Deshea | Devere |
| Denton | Design | Device |
| Denver | Designer | Devie |
| Denvo | Desijo | Deville |
| Denzel | Desin | Devin |
| Denzil | Desirae | Devina |
| Deole | Desire | Devine |
| Deon | Desiree | Devitt |
| Deondre | Desirée | Devo |
| Deonnah | Desmee | Devol |
| Deonte | Desmond | Devon |
| Depp | Desperado | Devona |
| Depuy | Dessange | Devonta |
| Dequan | Dessert | Devontae |
| Derby | Dessie | Devonte |

| | | |
|---|---|---|
| Devoted | Dickens | Dino |
| Devotion | Dickerson | Diola |
| Devra | Dickey | Dion |
| Devri | Dickie | Dionne |
| Devvyn | Dickinson | Dionte |
| Devyn | Diego | Diorio |
| Dew | Diek | Direct |
| Dewade | Diep | Dirk |
| Dewayne | Dierdre | Dirndl |
| Dewer | Dierick | Disc |
| Dewey | Diesel | Discover |
| Dewitt | Dieta | Discovery |
| Dewy | Dieter | Diseth |
| Dex | Dietrich | Distance |
| Dexee | Dietz | Divide |
| Dexter | Dietzway | Dividra |
| Deyette | Digger | Divina |
| Dezarae | Diggle | Dixie |
| Dezaray | Dijon | Dock |
| Dezi | Diker | Dodge |
| Dhaliwal | Dilaria | Dody |
| Diablo | Dillan | Doe |
| Dial | Dillard | Doland |
| Diamond | Diller | Dolena |
| Dian | Dilley | Doll |
| Diana | Dillion | Dollar |
| Diane | Dillon | Dollie |
| Diann | Dimitri | Dolly |
| Dianna | Dina | Dolores |
| Dianne | Dinah | Doloris |
| Dias | Dingui | Dolphin |
| Diaz | Dinh | Dome |
| Dibert | Dinneen | Domenic |
| Dick | Dinnetz | Domenica |

| | | |
|---|---|---|
| Domenick | Dooley | Dougal |
| Domenico | Door | Douglas |
| Dominador | Dora | Douglass |
| Dominga | Dorado | Dov |
| Domingo | Doran | Dove |
| Dominic | Dorathy | Dovea |
| Dominick | Dorcas | Dover |
| Dominique | Doreen | Dovie |
| Dominque | Dorene | Dow |
| Domonique | Doretha | Dowling |
| Don | Dori | Down |
| Dona | Dorian | Downer |
| Donal | Doric | Downey |
| Donald | Dorie | Downing |
| Donali | Dorinda | Downs |
| Donalli | Doris | Doyle |
| Donato | Dorit | Dozer |
| Donavan | Doro | Dozier |
| Dondra | Dorotha | Dragon |
| Donell | Dorothea | Drake |
| Dongho | Dorothy | Draper |
| Donia | Dorrie | Draw |
| Donita | Dorris | Drawjn |
| Donn | Dorsey | Drawn |
| Donna | Dortha | Drayson |
| Donnalee | Dorthy | Drayton |
| Donnell | Dorus | Drazil |
| Donner | Dory | Dream |
| Donnie | Dos | Drebick |
| Donny | Dosia | Dree |
| Donovan | Dot | Dreisbach |
| Donta | Dotson | Dresden |
| Dontae | Dottie | Dress |
| Donte | Doug | Dresser |

| | | |
|---|---|---|
| Dressor | Duke | Dust |
| Drestin | Dukes | Duster |
| Drew | Dulce | Duster |
| Drift | Dulcie | Dusti |
| Drifter | Dulin | Dustin |
| Drifton | Duluth | Dustine |
| Dristan | Dumas | Dusty |
| Driver | Dumlao | Dutch |
| Dru | Dumpert | Dutton |
| Drucilla | Duncan | Duvall |
| Dry | Dundee | Duwayne |
| Dryden | Dunedin | Duyungan |
| Drye | Dunham | Dwain |
| Du | Dunkin | Dwaine |
| Duane | Dunmore | Dwane |
| Dubb | Dunn | Dwayne |
| Dubigk | Dunnagan | Dweller |
| Dublin | Dunnock | Dwight |
| Dubois | Dunshee | Dwyer |
| Duby | Duquette | Dydemus |
| Ducat | Duran | Dye |
| Duck | Durango | Dyer |
| Duckett | Duren | Dykstra |
| Dudley | Durham | Dylan |
| Duey | Durk | Dylinn |
| Duff | Durrance | Dylon |
| Duffy | Durrin | Dyna |
| Dugan | Durst | Dysart |
| Dugay | Durward | Dyson |
| Dukakis | Duska | |

E is for "Everything" that you mean to me.
I'll prove this to you just wait and see.

| | | |
|---|---|---|
| Eagan | Easter | Ecklund |
| Eagen | Easterlin | Eclectic |
| Eagle | Eastern | Eclipse |
| Eakin | Eastham | Econ |
| Eakman | Eastman | Ed |
| Earl | Easton | Eda |
| Earle | Eaton | Edan |
| Earlean | Eave | Edd |
| Earlene | Ebba | Eddie |
| Earley | Ebel | Eddy |
| Earlie | Eberhart | Eden |
| Earline | Eberle | Edgar |
| Early | Ebey | Edgardo |
| Earnest | Eboni | Edge |
| Earnestine | Ebony | Edgewater |
| Earp | Ebrahim | Edie |
| Earth | Eccent | Edilberto |
| Eartha | Eccentric | Edina |
| Earthen | Echo | Edison |
| Earthtone | Echoe | Edita |
| East | Eckert | Edith |
| Easten | Eckley | Edler |

65

| | | |
|---|---|---|
| Edlon | Ehlers | Elder |
| Edmond | Ehlert | Eldon |
| Edmonds | Ehresmann | Eldora |
| Edmonton | Eicher | Eldred |
| Edmund | Eickmeyer | Eldridge |
| Edna | Eide | Eleanor |
| Edra | Eighth | Eleanora |
| Edralin | Eik | Eleanore |
| Edric | Eileen | Elease |
| Edrie | Einar | Elecktra |
| Edsel | Eino | Electa |
| Eduardo | Eirik | Electra |
| Edward | Ekenberg | Electric |
| Edwardo | Ekland | Elena |
| Edwards | Eklum | Elene |
| Edwin | Eklund | Elenor |
| Edwina | Ela | Elenora |
| Edyth | Eladio | Eleva |
| Edythe | Elaina | Eleven |
| Een | Elaine | Elfrieda |
| Effie | Elam | Elgharabli |
| Effort | Elan | Elgin |
| Efleda | Elana | Eli |
| Efrain | Elano | Elia |
| Efrem | Elara | Eliam |
| Efren | Elayne | Eliana |
| Egan | Elba | Elias |
| Egbert | Elbert | Elicia |
| Egg | Elbi | Eliezer |
| Eggar | Elcho | Eligio |
| Eggbert | Elcid | Eliiahu |
| Egolf | Eld | Elijah |
| Egon | Elda | Elim |
| Egypt | Elden | Eline |

| | | |
|---|---|---|
| Elinor | Elmore | Emanuel |
| Elinore | Elna | Emelia |
| Elion | Elnora | Emelie |
| Eliot | Eloheimo | Emerald |
| Eliou | Elois | Emerich |
| Elisa | Eloisa | Emerick |
| Elisabeth | Eloise | Emeron |
| Elise | Eloquent | Emerson |
| Eliseo | Elouise | Emery |
| Elisha | Eloy | Emil |
| Elissa | Elroy | Emile |
| Eliza | Elsa | Emilee |
| Elizabeth | Else | Emileigh |
| Ella | Elsie | Emilia |
| Ellamae | Elston | Emilie |
| Ellen | Elta | Emilio |
| Ellenton | Elton | Emily |
| Ellery | Elva | Emko |
| Elley | Elven | Emma |
| Elli | Elvera | Emmaline |
| Ellie | Elvie | Emmamorti |
| Ellingsen | Elvin | Emmano |
| Elliot | Elvira | Emmans |
| Elliott | Elvis | Emmanuel |
| Ellis | Elway | Emme |
| Ellory | Elwin | Emmet |
| Ellsworth | Elwood | Emmett |
| Ellwood | Elwyn | Emmie |
| Elm | Elyse | Emmit |
| Elma | Elyssa | Emmitt |
| Elmar | Elza | Emmons |
| Elmer | Elzie | Emmy |
| Elmira | Emamorte | Emogene |
| Elmo | Emamortea | Emory |

| | | |
|---|---|---|
| Empty | Enriqueta | Erinne |
| Emre | Ensley | Eris |
| Emry | Enter | Erleen |
| Ena | Entery | Erlene |
| Enders | Entire | Erley |
| Endia | Entry | Erling |
| Endora | Entsminger | Erma |
| Endura | Entwistle | Ermine |
| Eneas | Enya | Erna |
| Energy | Enyo | Ernest |
| Enfield | Eolande | Ernestina |
| Eng | Eon | Ernestine |
| Engel | Eors | Ernesto |
| Engelbert | Ephraim | Ernie |
| Engelhart | Ephron | Ernst |
| Enger | Eplin | Eros |
| Enges | Epperson | Errol |
| Engine | Equador | Erroll |
| England | Equator | Erskine |
| Engle | Era | Ervin |
| Engles | Eraser | Erving |
| English | Erastmus | Erwin |
| Englund | Erdahl | Erykah |
| Enid | Eriba | Esaias |
| Enlae | Eric | Esau |
| Enlow | Erica | Escude |
| Ennis | Erich | Eska |
| Enoch | Erick | Eslick |
| Enola | Ericka | Esme |
| Enos | Ericksen | Esmé |
| Enrica | Erickson | Esmeralda |
| Enrico | Erik | Esperanza |
| Enriqua | Erika | Espirit |
| Enrique | Erin | Esprit |

| | | |
|---|---|---|
| Esquimeaux | Ethel | Evans |
| Esra | Ethelene | Evant |
| Essence | Ethelred | Eve |
| Esser | Ethelyn | Evelinda |
| Essex | Etheridge | Eveline |
| Essie | Ethyl | Evelyn |
| Essture | Etienne | Evelyne |
| Esta | Etta | Even |
| Estate | Ettie | Evening |
| Esteban | Eubanks | Event |
| Estee | Euclid | Ever |
| Estefania | Eudora | Everest |
| Estel | Eugene | Everett |
| Estela | Eugenia | Everette |
| Estell | Eugenie | Everson |
| Estella | Eugenio | Evert |
| Estelle | Eula | Every |
| Estep | Eulah | Evette |
| Ester | Eulalia | E'Vette |
| Estes | Euna | Evie |
| Estevan | Eunice | Evon |
| Estey | Eura | Evonne |
| Esther | Eureka | Evra |
| Estrada | Euripides | Evva |
| Estrella | Europe | Evvie |
| Estus | Eusebio | Ewald |
| Eszhem | Eussen | Ewan |
| Etcetera | Eustace | Ewe |
| Etcheveria | Eva | Ewell |
| Etching | Evaline | Ewen |
| Eterna | Evalyn | Ewing |
| Eternity | Evan | Ewok |
| Etha | Evangelina | Ex |
| Ethan | Evangeline | Exam |

| | | |
|---|---|---|
| Excell | Exodus | Eyes |
| Excellence | Exotic | Eyvonne |
| Excellent | Expo | Eza |
| Exelby | Exposure | Ezekiel |
| Exie | Express | Ezeokeke |
| Exit | Exxon | Ezequiel |
| Exlipse | Eye | Ezra |

F is for "Fairytales" that I'll read to you.
Like Cinderella and Little Boy Blue.

| | | |
|---|---|---|
| Fabian | Fairley | Fame |
| Fabio | Fairview | Famous |
| Fabiola | Fairy | Fancher |
| Fable | Faison | Fane |
| Fabreeze | Faith | Fannie |
| Fabriz | Falcon | Fanning |
| Fabriza | Falina | Fanny |
| Fabry | Falis | Fanony |
| Face | Falk | Far |
| Fadden | Falkner | Fara |
| Fade | Falkowski | Faran |
| Fadel | Fall | Fargo |
| Fading | Fallahi | Farhad |
| Fae | Falle | Farid |
| Faechner | Falleen | Farina |
| Fagernes | Fallen | Faris |
| Fagley | Faller | Farivar |
| Fahning | Fallon | Farley |
| Fahoum | Fallow | Farm |
| Fail | Falls | Farmer |
| Fair | Falter | Farner |
| Fairbanks | Falyn | Farnsworth |

71

| | | |
|---|---|---|
| Faron | Fawnette | Felissa |
| Farrah | Fax | Felix |
| Farrar | Fay | Feliz |
| Farrel | Fayanne | Felke |
| Farrell | Faye | Fell |
| Farren | Fayek | Fellen |
| Farris | Fealy | Fellini |
| Farro | Feather | Fellow |
| Farrow | Featherstone | Felt |
| Farshid | Feature | Felton |
| Farson | February | Fence |
| Farzan | Federa | Fender |
| Fascination | Federal | Feniak |
| Fashion | Federation | Fennell |
| Fast | Federico | Fenner |
| Fasta | Fedora | Fenton |
| Fateen | Feeser | Feodora |
| Fatema | Feider | Fera |
| Fatima | Feighn | Feral |
| Fatou | Feil | Ferderer |
| Faul | Feisley | Ferdinand |
| Faulk | Feiten | Ferguson |
| Faulkner | Feivel | Ferie |
| Faulkton | Felecia | Ferluga |
| Faull | Felella | Fern |
| Fauna | Felenia | Fernald |
| Faunton | Felicia | Fernand |
| Faustina | Feliciano | Fernando |
| Faustino | Felicita | Ferne |
| Favor | Felicitie | Ferreira |
| Favorite | Felina | Ferrier |
| Fawcett | Felipa | Festiva |
| Fawn | Felipe | Fetch |
| Fawnda | Felisha | Fetterly |

| | | |
|---|---|---|
| Feury | Findley | Flagler |
| Fever | Finger | Flair |
| Fey | Finis | Flakner |
| Fialka | Fink | Flam |
| Fiber | Finkbeiner | Flame |
| Fibia | Finland | Flaming |
| Ficco | Finlay | Flamingo |
| Fiction | Finley | Flanders |
| Ficus | Finn | Flanigan |
| Fidel | Finnigan | Flannigan |
| Fidgeon | Finno | Flash |
| Field | Fiona | Flatulence |
| Fielding | Fionn | Flavin |
| Fields | Fir | Flaxton |
| Fierce | Firas | Fleckenstein |
| Fiero | Fire | Flector |
| Fiery | Fireday | Fledge |
| Fiesta | Firenze | Fleet |
| Fife | Firm | Fleetwood |
| Fifis | Firouzi | Fleming |
| Fifth | Fish | Flemming |
| Fig | Fisher | Fleta |
| Figg | Fisk | Fletch |
| Fighter | Fiske | Fletcher |
| Fiji | Fitch | Fleur |
| File | Fite | Fligh |
| Filip | Fitz | Flight |
| Filipe | Fitzgerald | Flint |
| Film | Fitzhugh | Flitter |
| Filomena | Fitzsimmons | Flo |
| Fina | Five | Flock |
| Final | Fix | Floor |
| Financier | Flack | Flopsy |
| Finch | Flag | Flora |

| | | |
|---|---|---|
| Floral | Fonda | Fostor |
| Florence | Fontana | Fouad |
| Florencio | Fontella | Four |
| Florene | Foor | Foushay |
| Florentino | Footprints | Fowler |
| Florian | For | Fox |
| Florida | Forbes | Foxton |
| Florine | Forbis | Foy |
| Florio | Ford | Foz |
| Floris | Fordjour | Frachiseur |
| Florist | Fordyce | Fraenzl |
| Florrie | Foreign | Fragrance |
| Flossi | Foreman | Fraley |
| Flossie | Foresman | Frame |
| Flow | Forest | Frames |
| Flower | Forever | Framesi |
| Floy | Forinash | Fran |
| Floyd | Form | France |
| Flue | Forrest | Frances |
| Fly | Forrist | Francesca |
| Flyer | Forst | Francesco |
| Flynn | Forster | Franchesca |
| Fodder | Fort | Francheska |
| Fog | Forte | Francine |
| Foister | Forth | Francis |
| Foisy | Fortner | Francisca |
| Foldger | Fortney | Francisco |
| Foley | Fortunate | Frank |
| Folgers | Fortunato | Frankie |
| Follett | Fortune | Frankle |
| Follis | Forza | Franklin |
| Follow | Foss | Frankly |
| Folsom | Fossil | Franklyn |
| Fomich | Foster | Franks |

| | | |
|---|---|---|
| Franz | Freezia | Frucci |
| Franzen | Freida | Frudd |
| Fraser | Freight | Fry |
| Frasier | Fremont | Frye |
| Frati | Frencesca | Fuda |
| Frazer | French | Fuel |
| Frazier | Frequent | Fuentes |
| Frazin | Fresh | Fujii |
| Fred | Fresno | Fulfs |
| Freda | Frey | Full |
| Freddie | Frick | Fuller |
| Freddy | Frida | Fullerton |
| Frederic | Friday | Fulton |
| Frederick | Frieda | Fumia |
| Fredericks | Friedrich | Fumii |
| Fredric | Friend | Fund |
| Fredrick | Frieze | Fung-Chen |
| Fredrickson | Fright | Funnel |
| Fredy | Frijos | Furlong |
| Free | Frisby | Furman |
| Freed | Frisco | Furrow |
| Freeda | Frissell | Furth |
| Freedom | Frithu | Furtune |
| Freedy | Fritz | Furu |
| Freeman | From | Fury |
| Freesia | Frost | Futon |
| Freeway | Frostad | Future |
| Freeze | Frosty | Fuzzy |
| Freezer | | |

G is for a little "Girl" sent from God above
A little soul he loaned to me, to care and give my love.

| | | |
|---|---|---|
| Gaasland | Gahan | Gallop |
| Gabe | Gail | Galloway |
| Gabel | Gailan | Galo |
| Gabera | Gailen | Galovic |
| Gable | Gaines | Gamal |
| Gabo | Gaiser | Gamb |
| Gabon | Gaius | Gamble |
| Gabriel | Gala | Gambol |
| Gabriela | Galadriel | Gamler |
| Gabriella | Galax | Ganden |
| Gabrielle | Galaxy | Gandy |
| Gacek | Gale | Gano |
| Gad | Galen | Garald |
| Gadd | Galer | Garcia |
| Gadge | Galera | Garden |
| Gadsen | Galinec | Gardener |
| Gadwa | Gallagher | Gardino |
| Gaetano | Gallalgher | Gardner |
| Gage | Gallant | Garett |
| Gagen | Gallery | Garfield |
| Gager | Gallinger | Garland |
| Gaham | Gallon | Garlington |

| | | |
|---|---|---|
| Garman | Gaylor | Genessa |
| Garner | Gaylord | Geneva |
| Garnes | Gaymon | Gene've |
| Garnet | Gaynor | Genevieve |
| Garnett | Gazelle | Genice |
| Garnson | Gear | Gennaro |
| Garold | Gearld | Gennie |
| Garret | Gearldine | Genny |
| Garrett | Geary | Genoa |
| Garrick | Geaudreau | Genova |
| Garrison | Gee | Genoveva |
| Garry | Geer | Gent |
| Garth | Geese | Gentle |
| Gartman | Gegen | Gentry |
| Garv | Gegoux | Geo |
| Garver | Gegu | Geoff |
| Garvin | Geia | Geoffrey |
| Garvy | Geier | George |
| Gary | Geiger | Georgette |
| Gasche | Geiser | Georgia |
| Gasparovich | Geltus | Georgiana |
| Gaston | Gemeni | Georgianna |
| Gate | Gemini | Georgie |
| Gates | Gena | Georgina |
| Gatlin | Genaro | Georgine |
| Gauge | Gency | Gerald |
| Gaven | Gene | Geraldine |
| Gavin | Geneive | Geraldo |
| Gay | Genelle | Geralyn |
| Gaye | Geneoa | Gerard |
| Gayla | General | Gerardo |
| Gayle | Generous | Gerbera |
| Gayleen | Generra | Gerda |
| Gaylon | Genesis | Geremy |

| | | |
|---|---|---|
| Gerhard | Gibson | Ginene |
| Geri | Giddon | Ginette |
| Geringer | Gideon | Ginger |
| Germaine | Gietz | Ginn |
| German | Gif | Ginnie |
| Germany | Giffin | Ginny |
| Gernhart | Gifford | Gino |
| Gerold | Gift | Ginoa |
| Gerri | Giggle | Ginter |
| Gerry | Gigi | Gion |
| Gersib | Gihring | Giordano |
| Gertie | Gil | Giorgio |
| Gertje | Gilad | Giovanna |
| Gertrude | Gilam | Giovanni |
| Gertson | Gilbert | Giovanny |
| Gervasio | Gilberto | Gipsy |
| Gervis | Gilchrist | Giraud |
| Gerwig | Gilda | Girl |
| Gerwyn | Giles | Girlie |
| Gets | Gilk | Giselle |
| Geylen | Gill | Gitchell |
| Geyser | Gillean | Gitel |
| Ghadamsi | Gillette | Gitter |
| Ghadeer | Gilliam | Giuseppe |
| Ghanie | Gillian | Given |
| Ghassan | Gilliatt | Gjuka |
| Ghebreghzabiher | Gillin | Glad |
| Ghent | Gillis | Gladden |
| Giancarlo | Gillispie | Glade |
| Gianna | Gilman | Gladsjo |
| Gianni | Gilmer | Glady |
| Gibbens | Gilroy | Gladyce |
| Gibbon | Gilson | Gladys |
| Gibbs | Gina | Gland |

| | | |
|---|---|---|
| Glas | Go | Goodman |
| Glasier | Gobi | Goodrich |
| Glasnost | Goble | Goose |
| Glass | Goche | Gord |
| Glassburn | Godfrey | Gorden |
| Glaze | Godin | Gordimer |
| Gleam | Godina | Gordon |
| Gleason | Goedge | Gordy |
| Gleckler | Goeres | Gorgana |
| Gleeson | Goffney | Gorge |
| Gleich | Golbek | Gorgeous |
| Glen | Gold | Gorski |
| Glenda | Golda | Goss |
| Glendon | Golden | Gosset |
| Glenn | Goldendale | Gossip |
| Glenna | Goldenrod | Gotcha |
| Glennie | Goldia | Goudarzi |
| Glennis | Goldie | Goudy |
| Gless | Goldin | Gough |
| Glessner | Goldsby | Gould |
| Glick | Goldstein | Gousse |
| Glidden | Golf | Gov |
| Glidewell | Golfer | Govan |
| Glimmer | Goller | Govanka |
| Glint | Golphenee | Governor |
| Glitter | Golson | Govlanko |
| Globe | Gombosky | Gow |
| Glondo | Gomes | Gowen |
| Gloor | Gone | Gower |
| Gloria | Gonia | Grabhorn |
| Glorilyn | Gonseth | Grace |
| Gluth | Gonzales | Gracie |
| Glynis | Gonzalo | Graciela |
| Glynn | Gooch | Grade |

| | | |
|---|---|---|
| Grady | Graysen | Gresham |
| Graeber | Grayson | Greta |
| Graeme | Grayton | Gretchen |
| Graft | Graz | Grettenberg |
| Grafton | Great | Grey |
| Graham | Greate | Greyling |
| Grail | Greatly | Greysen |
| Gram | Greatorex | Greyson |
| Granbois | Grecian | Gribbin |
| Grand | Greco | Gribner |
| Grande | Greebey | Griesbaum |
| Grandorff | Greece | Griff |
| Grandsen | Greek | Griffen |
| Grange | Greeley | Griffey |
| Granger | Green | Griffin |
| Granita | Greene | Griffith |
| Granite | Greenfield | Grifton |
| Grant | Greenlee | Grigori |
| Grantham | Greensburo | Grigware |
| Grantley | Greenwood | Grillo |
| Granville | Greer | Grimalkin |
| Gras | Greetus | Grimes |
| Grass | Greg | Grimm |
| Gravel | Gregerson | Grimmett |
| Gravelly | Gregg | Grin |
| Graven | Greggory | Grinaker |
| Graves | Gregoire | Grinnell |
| Gravity | Gregor | Gripen |
| Gravlin | Gregoria | Gris |
| Gravy | Gregorio | Grisby |
| Gray | Gregorios | Griselda |
| Graybill | Gregory | Griss |
| Grayce | Gregson | Gristin |
| Grayland | Gren | Griswald |

| | | |
|---|---|---|
| Griswold | Gugan | Gussie |
| Grizzley | Guide | Gust |
| Groat | Guido | Gustafsson |
| Groh | Guillemma | Gustav |
| Groove | Guillermin | Gustave |
| Groth | Guillermo | Gustavo |
| Ground | Guinn | Gustine |
| Grove | Guinotte | Gutema |
| Grover | Guiseppe | Guthrie |
| Grubb | Guiser | Gutierrez |
| Gruber | Gull | Guttormsen |
| Gruenberg | Gullekson | Guy |
| Gruenhagen | Gum | Guyant |
| Gruginski | Gun | Guyton |
| Guadaloupe | Gunderson | Gwen |
| Guadalupe | Gunn | Gwendolyn |
| Guam | Gunnar | Gwenn |
| Guard | Gunner | Gwilym |
| Guardian | Gunter | Gwo |
| Gubbe | Gunther | Gwyneth |
| Gucci | Guorong | Gwynne |
| Gudrun | Guptill | Gylland |
| Guerrero | Gurbachan | Gym |
| Guess | Gurule | Gymnasia |
| Guest | Gus | Gypsy |

H is for "Happiness" that you'll bring into our home.
You'll always be loved and never alone.

| | | |
|---|---|---|
| Ha | Haeger | Hain |
| Haag | Haeline | Hainault |
| Haakon | Hafer | Haiti |
| Haan | Haffie | Haivana |
| Haapala | Hagar | Hake |
| Hachmeister | Hagbo | Hakeem |
| Hack | Hagedorn | Hakes |
| Hacker | Hagen | Hakola |
| Hackford | Hager | Hal |
| Hackman | Haggard | Haldon |
| Hackworth | Haggarety | Hale |
| Haddam | Hagglund | Haledon |
| Haddaway | Hahn | Haleigh |
| Hadden | Hai | Haley |
| Haddock | Haiden | Hali |
| Hade | Haider | Halie |
| Haden | Haigh | Halifax |
| Hadfield | Haight | Halimah |
| Hadley | Hailee | Halk |
| Hadlock | Hailey | Hall |
| Hadrian | Haili | Hallam |
| Haecherl | Haim | Hallauer |

| | | |
|---|---|---|
| Halle | Hampton | Hardy |
| Hallead | Hamre | Harger |
| Halley | Hams | Hargrove |
| Hallford | Hamson | Harjit |
| Hallie | Hana | Hark |
| Halloween | Hanchinamani | Harlan |
| Hallowell | Hancock | Harlequin |
| Hallsted | Handi | Harley |
| Halsman | Haner | Harlo |
| Halt | Haney | Harlow |
| Halton | Hank | Harmon |
| Halverson | Hankins | Harmony |
| Halverstadt | Hanley | Harold |
| Halvorson | Hanna | Harper |
| Halvy | Hannah | Harriet |
| Hamacher | Hanni | Harriett |
| Hamadeh | Hanning | Harriette |
| Hamblet | Hannomag | Harris |
| Hambrick | Hannon | Harrison |
| Hamden | Hans | Harrow |
| Hame | Hansel | Harry |
| Hamid | Hansen | Harshman |
| Hamil | Hanshew | Harston |
| Hamilton | Hanson | Hart |
| Hamlet | Happy | Hartford |
| Hamlin | Harald | Hartill |
| Hamma | Harbor | Hartley |
| Hammack | Harbors | Hartman |
| Hammel | Harden | Hartsell |
| Hammer | Hardie | Hartsfield |
| Hammersmith | Hardin | Hartstrom |
| Hammond | Harding | Hartwell |
| Hamp | Hardtke | Harvard |
| Hampden | Hardway | Harvest |

| | | |
|---|---|---|
| Harvey | Haupt | Haze |
| Hasan | Hausa | Hazel |
| Hash | Havalina | Hazelton |
| Hashemi | Havana | Hazen |
| Hasina | Havanna | Hazie |
| Haskell | Havasota | Hazle |
| Haskey | Havelina | Hazy |
| Haslam | Haven | Hazzard |
| Hassan | Havent | Hazzouk |
| Hasselbach | Haveri | Hea |
| Hassen | Haviland | Heale |
| Hassie | Havlin | Healey |
| Haste | Havlina | Healy |
| Hasten | Hawaii | Heard |
| Hastine | Hawes | Hearne |
| Hasting | Hawk | Heart |
| Hastings | Hawke | Heat |
| Hasty | Hawkes | Heath |
| Hatch | Hawkins | Heathcliff |
| Hatcher | Hay | Heather |
| Hatfield | Haydee | Heatherly |
| Hatford | Hayden | Heathman |
| Hathaway | Hayes | Heaton |
| Hatley | Haylee | Heaven |
| Hattan | Hayley | Heavenly |
| Hattie | Haylie | Heavensent |
| Hatton | Hayman | Hebatallah |
| Hau | Haynal | Heber |
| Haugen | Hayner | Hebrides |
| Haugness | Haynes | Hec |
| Haukap | Hays | Heckard |
| Hauke | Hayward | Hector |
| Haul | Haywood | Hedden |
| Haun | Hayworth | Heden |

| | | |
|---|---|---|
| Hedin | Hellman | Hepburn |
| Hedrick | Hello | Hepler |
| Hedwig | Helma | Her |
| Hegge | Helmann | Hera |
| Hegyi | Helmer | Herbert |
| Heide | Helms | Herd |
| Heiden | Helmsley | Heriberto |
| Heidenrich | Helmsman | Heritage |
| Heidi | Helvey | Herizion |
| Heifer | Hembury | Herland |
| Height | Heming | Herman |
| Heigl | Hemming | Hermann |
| Heikkila | Hemp | Hermina |
| Heil | Hendersen | Hermine |
| Heildago | Henderson | Herminia |
| Heilman | Hendrick | Herminio |
| Hein | Hendricks | Hermod |
| Heinley | Hendrickson | Hermon |
| Heinold | Hendrix | Herna |
| Heinrich | Henke | Hernan |
| Heins | Henkel | Hernandez |
| Heintz | Henley | Herndon |
| Heinz | Hennessy | Hero |
| Heinze | Hennigh | Herod |
| Heitzenrader | Henning | Heron |
| Heitzman | Henri | Herrera |
| Heizenrader | Henrietta | Herrington |
| Helen | Henriette | Herrmann |
| Helena | Henrikson | Herron |
| Helene | Henry | Herschel |
| Helga | Henryk | Hershel |
| Helge | Henselman | Herst |
| Helland | Hensley | Hert |
| Hellen | Henson | Herta |

Herth
Hertha
Hertis
Hertzog
Hervé
Heryford
Hess
Hessen
Hester
Hesterberg
Heston
Hettie
Heureux
Hevener
Hevy
Hewitt
Hezekiah
Hicks
Hidden
Hider
Hien
Hiep
Hieu
Higdon
Higgins
High
Highland
Hike
Hilario
Hilary
Hilbert
Hilda
Hilde
Hildegard

Hildegarde
Hilding
Hildred
Hildur
Hill
Hillan
Hillard
Hillary
Hille
Hiller
Hilliard
Hillie
Hillion
Hills
Hillsman
Hilly
Hilma
Hilmes
Hilse
Hilsinger
Hilton
Hilts
Himalaya
Himmel
Hiner
Hines
Hinge
Hinkle
Hinson
Hintley
Hinton
Hinzmann
Hipolito
Hiram

Hirzel
Historia
History
Hitch
Hitzke
Hix
Hjelmeseth
Ho
Hoa
Hoagland
Hoang
Hobart
Hobbs
Hobert
Hobi
Hobson
Hockett
Hoctor
Hodel
Hodge
Hoeinghaus
Hoff
Hoffam
Hoffer
Hoffine
Hoffman
Hogan
Hogg
Hogue
Hokanson
Holbrock
Holbrook
Hold
Holden

| | | |
|---|---|---|
| Holder | Hon | Horwitz |
| Holding | Hona | Hosaia |
| Holdren | Honda | Hose |
| Holiday | Honest | Hosea |
| Holister | Honestly | Hoseb |
| Hollan | Honesty | Hosek |
| Holland | Honey | Hoser |
| Hollander | Hongzhi | Hosey |
| Hollenbeck | Honheur | Hosie |
| Holli | Honor | Hosler |
| Hollie | Honsinger | Hour |
| Hollis | Hook | Houshman |
| Holly | Hooper | Houston |
| Hollydae | Hoover | Houx |
| Holm | Hope | Hovda |
| Holman | Hopkins | Hovde |
| Holmes | Hops | Hovland |
| Holmquist | Hoquiam | Howard |
| Holmstrom | Horace | Howden |
| Holster | Horacio | Howe |
| Holstine | Horatio | Howell |
| Holston | Horaz | Howie |
| Holt | Horizon | Howitzer |
| Holte | Horizontal | Howsie |
| Holten | Horlacher | Howson |
| Holtermann | Horman | Howzer |
| Holttum | Horn | Howzit |
| Holtz | Horne | Hoy |
| Holy | Horse | Hoyos |
| Holze | Horst | Hoyt |
| Hom | Hortense | Hozey |
| Homan | Hortensia | Hristo |
| Home | Hortin | Hros |
| Homer | Horton | Hsieh |

| | | |
|---|---|---|
| Hua | Hull | Hurt |
| Hubbard | Hulme | Husain |
| Huber | Hulse | Hussel |
| Hubert | Hulzebos | Hussey |
| Huck | Humberto | Hustle |
| Hud | Hume | Huston |
| Hudgins | Hummel | Hutch |
| Hudson | Humphrey | Hutchenson |
| Huether | Humphreys | Hutchine |
| Huey | Hun | Hutchinson |
| Huff | Hung | Hutchison |
| Huffman | Hunt | Hutten |
| Hufton | Huntamer | Hutton |
| Hug | Hunter | Huynh |
| Hugdahl | Hunterdon | Hyatt |
| Hugg | Huntington | Hyde |
| Hugger | Huntley | Hydra |
| Hugh | Hurch | Hye |
| Hughes | Hurd | Hylan |
| Hugo | Hurdle | Hylebos |
| Hulbert | Hurricane | Hynek |
| Hulda | Hursh | Hyp |
| Hulk | Hurst | Hyrum |

I is for "Intelligence" that you gain as you grow up.
From crawling and talking to sipping a cup.

| | | |
|---|---|---|
| Iaegar | Icie | Ikari |
| Iagger | Icy | Ikatan |
| Iain | Ida | Ike |
| Iakov | Idaho | Ikea |
| Ian | Idalia | Ikehara |
| Iana | Idan | Ikenberry |
| Ianada | Idanha | Ila |
| Iani | Ideal | Ilan |
| Iantha | Idell | Ilana |
| Iay | Idella | Ilea |
| Ibaden | Identity | Ileana |
| Ibe | Idest | Ilene |
| Iben | Idkeidek | Iler |
| Iberia | Idol | Iliana |
| Ibid | Idra | Illahee |
| Ibrahim | Iesha | Illg |
| Ice | Ieuan | Illinois |
| Iceland | Ifan | Ima |
| Icelandia | Ignacio | Iman |
| Ich | Igor | Imani |
| Ichabod | Ii | Imara |
| Ichelle | Iii | Imari |

| | | |
|---|---|---|
| Imelda | Ingrid | Irwin |
| Imhof | Inks | Isaac |
| Immel | Inky | Isabel |
| Imogene | Inn | Isabell |
| Imran | Innes | Isabella |
| Ina | Inspiration | Isabelle |
| Inaline | Instant | Isadore |
| Inari | Integrity | Isai |
| Incub | Ioa | Isaiah |
| Independence | Iola | Isaias |
| Independent | Iolanda | Isak |
| Inder | Iolande | Isamar |
| India | Ion | Isao |
| Indiana | Iona | Isas |
| Indigo | Ione | Isela |
| Indio | Iota | Iselton |
| Indore | Iov | Isherwood |
| Indra | Iowa | Ishmael |
| Indri | Ipava | Isiah |
| Ineka | Ira | Isidore |
| Ines | Iran | Isidro |
| Ine's | Iraq | Isis |
| Inez | Ire | Island |
| Inga | Ireka | Islay |
| Ingall | Ireland | Isle |
| Ingalls | Irene | Isles |
| Inge | Irilla | Isleta |
| Ingeborg | Irina | Ismael |
| Inger | Iris | Isobel |
| Ingersoll | Irma | Isom |
| Ingo | Irney | Israel |
| Ingra | Iron | Isringhaus |
| Ingraham | Irvin | Issa |
| Ingram | Irving | Issac |

| Issam | Ivar | Ivy |
| Itai | Ive | Izaack |
| Italia | Ivelisse | Izaak |
| Italy | Iverson | Izack |
| Itasca | Ives | Izador |
| Item | Ivette | Izeck |
| Ithaca | Ivey | Izetta |
| Ithia | Ivo | Izidor |
| Itzel | Ivon | Izigan |
| Iva | Ivonne | Izora |
| Ivah | Ivor | Izydor |
| Ivan | Ivory | Izzy |
| Ivanhoe | | |

J is for "Jesus," he'll protect you, I pray.
And he will watch over you every step of the way.

| | | |
|---|---|---|
| Jab | Jacob | Jael |
| Jabari | Jacobs | Jaelyn |
| Jabbar | Jacobsen | Jaga |
| Jabe | Jacobson | Jaggar |
| Jabez | Jacoby | Jagger |
| Jabin | Jacque | Jaguar |
| Jabon | Jacquelin | Jahmal |
| Jac | Jacqueline | Jahmil |
| Jace | Jacquelyn | Jai |
| Jacett | Jacques | Jaime |
| Jacey | Jacquie | Jaimie |
| Jaci | Jacquline | Jair |
| Jacinda | Jacy | Jairo |
| Jacinto | Jacynda | Jairus |
| Jack | Jada | Jaison |
| Jackal | Jade | Jake |
| Jackie | Jadee | Jakob |
| Jacklyn | Jaden | Jalalyar |
| Jackman | Jadey | Jalapeno |
| Jackson | Jadon | Jalean |
| Jacky | Jaeg | Jaleel |
| Jaclyn | Jaegar | Jalen |

| | | |
|---|---|---|
| Jalil | Janeá | Jaron |
| Jalina | Janeen | Jarred |
| Jalisa | Janel | Jarrell |
| Jalita | Janell | Jarret |
| Jamaal | Janelle | Jarrett |
| Jamaica | Janessa | Jarrod |
| Jamaican | Janet | Jartan |
| Jamail | Janette | Jarvis |
| Jamaine | Jani | Jary |
| Jamal | Janice | Jase |
| Jamar | Janie | Jasen |
| Jamarcus | Janiero | Jasha |
| Jamari | Janine | Jashinski |
| Jame | Janis | Jasmeen |
| Jamel | Janka | Jasmin |
| James | Janna | Jasmine |
| Jameson | Jannette | Jason |
| Jamey | Jannie | Jasper |
| Jameyson | Janosky | Jassen |
| Jami | Jansen | Jasson |
| Jamie | Janson | Jasteal |
| Jamieson | Jantz | Jastiel |
| Jamil | Jantzen | Jastra |
| Jamila | January | Jauffman |
| Jamison | Janus | Jaunita |
| Jammie | Japan | Javalina |
| Jan | Japanese | Javano |
| Jana | Jaquan | Javeline |
| Janaa | Jaqueline | Javi |
| Janacek | Jarah | Javier |
| Janae | Jared | Javins |
| Janay | Jarek | Javod |
| Jandria | Jarnail | Javon |
| Jane | Jarod | Javonte |

| | | |
|---|---|---|
| Javy | Jean-Pierre | Jennifer |
| Jay | Jed | Jennings |
| Jayden | Jeddy | Jennipher |
| Jaydon | Jedediah | Jenny |
| Jayla | Jedidiah | Jeno |
| Jaylen | Jeel | Jensen |
| Jaylin | Jeff | Jensi |
| Jaylon | Jefferey | Jenson |
| Jayme | Jeffers | Jepperson |
| Jaymee | Jefferson | Jerad |
| Jaymir | Jeffery | Jerald |
| Jayna | Jeffrey | Jeramie |
| Jayne | Jeffreys | Jeramy |
| Jaynee | Jeffry | Jere |
| Jayson | Jehna | Jered |
| Jayton | Jelani | Jerel |
| Jazmeen | Jelly | Jeremey |
| Jazmin | Jemez | Jeremiah |
| Jazmine | Jena | Jeremie |
| Jazmyn | Jenah | Jeremy |
| Jazon | Jen-Chi | Jeri |
| Jazz | Jenda | Jeriah |
| Jean | Jene | Jericho |
| Jeana | Jenelle | Jerick |
| Jeane | Jenesse | Jerilee |
| Jeanette | Jenifer | Jerill |
| Jeanie | Jenkins | Jerleen |
| Jeanine | Jenks | Jermain |
| Jean-Luc | Jenn | Jermaine |
| Jeanna | Jenna | Jermey |
| Jeanne | Jennene | Jerod |
| Jeannette | Jenner | Jerold |
| Jeannie | Jennette | Jerome |
| Jeannine | Jennie | Jeromy |

| | | |
|---|---|---|
| Jerou | Jetta | Joanne |
| Jerrell | Jettie | Joaquin |
| Jerrett | Jevon | Jobe |
| Jerri | Jewel | Joblonski |
| Jerric | Jewelianne | Jocelyn |
| Jerrica | Jewell | Jocinda |
| Jerrod | Jewett | Jodelle |
| Jerrold | Jex | Jodena |
| Jerry | Jez | Jodi |
| Jersey | Jhanna | Jodie |
| Jerzie | Jick | Jodine |
| Jeshuah | Jierine | Jody |
| Jesica | Jig | Joe |
| Jeslyn | Jiggle | Joel |
| Jess | Jihlette | Joell |
| Jesse | Jilayne | Jo-Ellan |
| Jessee | Jill | Joelle |
| Jessenia | Jillian | Jo-Ellen |
| Jessey | Jim | Joemma |
| Jessi | Jime | Joesph |
| Jessica | Jimmie | Joey |
| Jessie | Jimmy | Johann |
| Jessika | Jina | Johanna |
| Jessup | Jines | Johathan |
| Jessy | Jinjur | Johaunna |
| Jestile | Jinnie | John |
| Jestina | Jinny | John Henry |
| Jesus | Jiri | John Paul |
| Jesusa | Jo | Johna |
| Jet | Joachim | Johnasen |
| Jethro | Joan | Johnassa |
| Jetina | Joana | Johnathan |
| Jets | Joann | Johnathon |
| Jett | Joanna | Johnie |

| | | |
|---|---|---|
| Johnna | Joni | Joslin |
| Johnnie | Jonna | Joslyn |
| Johnny | Jonnie | Jostle |
| Johns | Jonny | Josue |
| Johnson | Joolz | Jourdain |
| Johnston | Joop | Journal |
| Johnstone | Joost | Journey |
| Johrden | Joplin | Jovan |
| Join | Jopplin | Jovanka |
| Joji | Jordan | Jovanny |
| Joker | Jorden | Jovanovich |
| Joleá | Jordon | Jovany |
| Joleé | Jordyn | Jovi |
| Jolene | Jorge | Joy |
| Joletta | Jorgensen | Joyce |
| Jolie | Jorgenson | Joyella |
| Joline | Jorin | Jozef |
| Jollie | Jorintha | Jr |
| Jolly | Jos | Juan |
| Jomar | Jose | Juana |
| Jomo | Joseb | Juanita |
| Jon | Joseelyn | Juanito |
| Jona | Josef | Juba |
| Jonah | Josefa | Jubal |
| Jonas | Josefina | Jubitz |
| Jonassa | Joselyn | Judas |
| Jonatan | Joseph | Judd |
| Jonathan | Josephine | Jude |
| Jonathon | Josette | Judge |
| Jones | Josh | Judi |
| Jonesha | Joshua | Judie |
| Jonessa | Joshuah | Judith |
| Jonesta | Josiah | Judson |
| Jong | Josie | Judy |

| | | |
|---|---|---|
| Jugesh | Julio | Jura |
| Juggler | Julissa | Jurasin |
| Jules | Julius | Juris |
| Juli | July | Jury |
| Julia | Jump | Justen |
| Julian | Jumper | Justice |
| Juliana | June | Justin |
| Juliann | Juneau | Justina |
| Julianna | Junett | Justine |
| Julianne | Jung | Juston |
| Juliano | Junior | Justus |
| Julie | Junious | Justyn |
| Julien | Juniper | Jute |
| Juliet | Junius | Juul |
| Juliette | Jupiter | Juwan |

K is for "Kisses" just for you.
Remember I'm here when you're feeling blue.

| | | |
|---|---|---|
| Kaake | Kagi | Kakada |
| Kabe | Kahill | Kake |
| Kacey | Kahla | Kala |
| Kaci | Kai | Kalahari |
| Kacie | Kai Lea | Kalamath |
| Kacy | Kaid | Kalani |
| Kade | Kaiden | Kalannie |
| Kadeem | Kaila | Kaleb |
| Kaden | Kailea | Kalee |
| Kado | Kailean | Kaleidos |
| Kadoka | Kailee | Kaleigh |
| Kadz | Kailey | Kalen |
| Kae | Kaily | Kalena |
| Kaech | Kailyn | Kaley |
| Kael | Kain | Kalgin |
| Kaela | Kaine | Kali |
| Kaelan | Kairo | Kalida |
| Kaelea | Kaiser | Kalie |
| Kaelie | Kaiska | Kalin |
| Kaemon | Kaitlin | Kalisch |
| Kaena | Kaitlyn | Kalkwarf |
| Kaeto | Kaitlynn | Kalle |

| | | |
|---|---|---|
| Kallen | Kansas | Karly |
| Kallevig | Kantu | Karma |
| Kallie | Kanye | Karmel |
| Kalona | Kanyon | Karol |
| Kalska | Kao | Karri |
| Kaltag | Kaori | Karrie |
| Kalvin | Kaplan | Karrington |
| Kalyn | Kapur | Karson |
| Kam | Kara | Karsonette |
| Kamal | Karam | Karst |
| Kamali | Karami | Karsten |
| Kamara | Karan | Karta |
| Kameron | Karat | Karthen |
| Kami | Kareem | Kartnen |
| Kamilla | Kareena | Karyn |
| Kamilli | Karen | Kasandra |
| Kamp | Karensa | Kasey |
| Kamran | Kari | Kash |
| Kamri | Karia | Kashan |
| Kamryn | Karie | Kashani |
| Kana | Karienne | Kashe |
| Kanaia | Karin | Kashmar |
| Kance | Karina | Kashtan |
| Kandace | Karis | Kasim |
| Kandi | Karissa | Kaskey |
| Kandice | Karita | Kaskin |
| Kandie | Karl | Kason |
| Kandis | Karla | Kasper |
| Kandy | Karlee | Kassa |
| Kandyce | Karlene | Kassandra |
| Kane | Karlenna | Kassidy |
| Kanga | Karley | Kassie |
| Kano | Karli | Kasson |
| Kanosh | Karlie | Kastama |

| | | |
|---|---|---|
| Kastner | Katrena | Kaylyn |
| Kat | Katrice | Kaylynn |
| Katalinich | Katrina | Kazan |
| Katan | Kattie | Kaze |
| Katania | Katts | Kazie |
| Katarina | Katy | Ke Lanié |
| Kate | Katz | Keahau |
| Katelin | Katzar | Keanu |
| Katelyn | Katzen | Keaton |
| Katelynn | Katzer | Kebble |
| Katerina | Kauai | Kebra |
| Kathan | Kaufman | Kecia |
| Katharina | Kautz | Keech |
| Katharine | Kauzloric | Keegan |
| Katherine | Kava | Keel |
| Katheryn | Kavage | Keeler |
| Katheu | Kavaila | Keeley |
| Kathi | Kavala | Keelie |
| Kathie | Kavali | Keely |
| Kathleen | Kavi | Keen |
| Kathlyn | Kavli | Keena |
| Kathrina | Kavola | Keenan |
| Kathrine | Kay | Keep |
| Kathryn | Kaycee | Keepers |
| Kathryne | Kayden | Keepsake |
| Kathy | Kaye | Keesha |
| Kati | Kayla | Keeta |
| Katia | Kaylah | Keeton |
| Katie | Kaylee | Kegal |
| Katijo | Kayleigh | Kegan |
| Katina | Kayley | Kehn |
| Katlin | Kayli | Kei |
| Katlyn | Kaylie | Keifenheim |
| Katlynn | Kaylin | Keifer |

| | | |
|---|---|---|
| Keil | Kelsie | Kenora |
| Keila | Kelso | Kenosha |
| Keir | Kelsy | Kensington |
| Keira | Kelsye | Kensrud |
| Keiser | Kelton | Kenstowicz |
| Keisha | Kelvin | Kent |
| Keishla | Kembie | Kenton |
| Keita | Kemble | Kentuckey |
| Keith | Kemp | Kenworth |
| Keizer | Kemper | Kenya |
| Kelani | Kempton | Kenyatta |
| Kelannie | Ken | Kenyon |
| Kelaso | Kendal | Kenzington |
| Kelby | Kendall | Keomarie |
| Kelcie | Kendegy | Keon |
| Kele | Kendell | Keonitzer |
| Kellar | Kendle | Keono |
| Kelleher | Kendol | Kepler |
| Kellen | Kendra | Kera |
| Keller | Kendrick | Keren |
| Kellerman | Kenerly | Kergi |
| Kelley | Kengo | Keri |
| Kelli | Kenia | Kermit |
| Kellie | Keniston | Kern |
| Kelln | Kenna | Kerns |
| Kellogg | Kennaugh | Kerr |
| Kelly | Kennedy | Kerri |
| Ké Loni | Kenneta | Kerrian |
| Ké Lonnie | Kenneth | Kerrie |
| Ké Lony | Kenney | Kerrigan |
| Kelowna | Kennington | Kerrington |
| Kelsea | Kennith | Kerry |
| Kelsey | Kennth | Kerschner |
| Kelsi | Kenny | Kersen |

| | | |
|---|---|---|
| Kershaw | Khris | Kilmer |
| Kerslake | Khue | Kilpatrick |
| Kerstie | Ki | Kilseimer |
| Kerstin | Kia | Kilt |
| Kerwin | Kiana | Kiltie |
| Kesha | Kianna | Kim |
| Keshia | Kiara | Kimball |
| Kesia | Kiave | Kimberlee |
| Kesler | Kibby | Kimberley |
| Kessler | Kidda | Kimberli |
| Ketchum | Kidder | Kimberlin |
| Kettle | Kiddo | Kimberly |
| Keven | Kidwell | Kimbrel |
| Kevin | Kiefer | Kimes |
| Kevon | Kiehn | Kimisha |
| Key | Kiel | Kimmel |
| Keya | Kienbaum | Kimmy |
| Keyes | Kieninger | Kimo |
| Keylany | Kienna | Kin |
| Keys | Kientra | Kincy |
| Keyze | Kientz | Kind |
| Keyzers | Kiera | Kindell |
| Kezzie | Kierah | Kinder |
| Khadijah | Kieran | Kinderman |
| Khaleghi | Kierra | Kindle |
| Khalid | Kiersten | Kindler |
| Khalil | Kija | Kindom |
| Khalili | Kiki | Kindy |
| Khamouan | Kiko | Kineisha |
| Khan | Kikol | King |
| Khanh | Kilamanjaro | Kingdom |
| Khara | Kilen | Kingdon |
| Khodr | Kiley | Kingman |
| Khoi | Killaby | Kingsley |

| | | |
|---|---|---|
| Kingston | Kirstianni | Klemens |
| Kinion | Kirstie | Klementine |
| Kinne | Kirstin | Kletch |
| Kinney | Kirsty | Klett |
| Kinsella | Kirt | Klinck |
| Kinser | Kirte | Kline |
| Kinsey | Kirton | Klinge |
| Kinskey | Kisch | Klinger |
| Kinsman | Kisha | Klingman |
| Kinswa | Kiska | Knaebel |
| Kinter | Kismet | Knapp |
| Kintner | Kistler | Knavel |
| Kintu | Kit | Knawa |
| Kinyan | Kite | Knecht |
| Kioshi | Kitsap | Kneeland |
| Kip | Kitten | Knight |
| Kipling | Kittie | Knipfer |
| Kipp | Kitty | Knisley |
| Kira | Kiva | Knittle |
| Kirby | Kiwi | Knopp |
| Kiri | Kiyoshi | Knott |
| Kirk | Kizzy | Knowlen |
| Kirkemo | Kjell | Knox |
| Kirkendall | Kjerstin | Knuckey |
| Kirker | Kjos | Knudsen |
| Kirkland | Klaas | Knudson |
| Kirkwood | Klamath | Knutson |
| Kirl | Klara | Koala |
| Kirle | Klasell | Kobe |
| Kirner | Klass | Kobi |
| Kiro | Klaudia | Koby |
| Kirsch | Klaus | Kobza |
| Kirslyn | Klech | Kodac |
| Kirsten | Klein | Kode |

| | | |
|---|---|---|
| Koden | Kook | Kreger |
| Kodiak | Koontz | Kreidler |
| Kody | Kopachuck | Krengel |
| Koen | Koperek | Kress |
| Koenig | Korbut | Kreuger |
| Kofi | Korby | Krieger |
| Kofstad | Korea | Kriewald |
| Kogin | Koreski | Krikava |
| Kohaunna | Korey | Kris |
| Kohl | Kori | Krisa |
| Kohlam | Korina | Krisandra |
| Kohler | Kortez | Krishna |
| Kohlhase | Kortney | Krislyn |
| Kohl-Welles | Kortnie | Krist |
| Koidal | Kortum | Krista |
| Koin | Kory | Kristal |
| Kojo | Kosa | Kristan |
| Kokomo | Kosinskaya | Kristen |
| Kolas | Koski | Kristi |
| Kolby | Kourtney | Kristian |
| Kole | Kov | Kristiansen |
| Kolle | Kovac | Kristie |
| Koller | Kovach | Kristin |
| Kollman | Kovich | Kristina |
| Kolsa | Koy | Kristine |
| Kolter | Kraemer | Kristofer |
| Kolton | Kraft | Kristoffer |
| Komac | Krahenbuhl | Kristopher |
| Kon-Lee | Kraig | Kristrom |
| Kona | Kramer | Kristy |
| Konek | Kraus | Kristyn |
| Konelly | Krause | Kristynna |
| Konnor | Kravis | Krocker |
| Konrad | Kreg | Kroger |

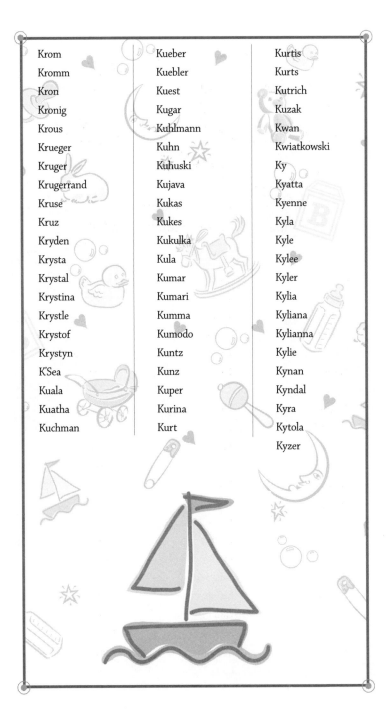

| | | |
|---|---|---|
| Krom | Kueber | Kurtis |
| Kromm | Kuebler | Kurts |
| Kron | Kuest | Kutrich |
| Kronig | Kugar | Kuzak |
| Krous | Kuhlmann | Kwan |
| Krueger | Kuhn | Kwiatkowski |
| Kruger | Kuhuski | Ky |
| Krugerrand | Kujava | Kyatta |
| Kruse | Kukas | Kyenne |
| Kruz | Kukes | Kyla |
| Kryden | Kukulka | Kyle |
| Krysta | Kula | Kylee |
| Krystal | Kumar | Kyler |
| Krystina | Kumari | Kylia |
| Krystle | Kumma | Kyliana |
| Krystof | Kumodo | Kylianna |
| Krystyn | Kuntz | Kylie |
| K'Sea | Kunz | Kynan |
| Kuala | Kuper | Kyndal |
| Kuatha | Kurina | Kyra |
| Kuchman | Kurt | Kytola |
| | | Kyzer |

L is for "Love" most important of all.
Without it we wilt, stumble and fall.

| | | |
|---|---|---|
| La | Ladarius | Lagerberg |
| Laar | Ladd | Lagergren |
| Laars | Ladder | Lagerquist |
| Laarsen | Laddie | Lagger |
| Laban | Ladelle | Lagoberto |
| Labay | Ladeye | Lahaie |
| Labolle | Ladleton | Lahd |
| Laborn | Ladner | Lahti |
| Labranche | Ladonia | Laiciano |
| Labrash | Ladonna | Laidler |
| Labreck | Ladue | Laik |
| Lacacia | Lady | Laika |
| Lacey | Lael | Laila's |
| Laci | Laeth | Lailia's |
| Lacie | Laetisia | Laine |
| Lackey | Laetitia | Lainel |
| Lacon | Lafayette | Laing |
| Laconner | Lafferty | Lainy |
| Lacoy | Lafond | Lair |
| Lacroix | Laforest | Lairs |
| Lacy | Lafoust | Laira |
| Lad | Lager | Laird |

106

| | | |
|---|---|---|
| Lais | Lanctot | Lani |
| Laisan | Land | Lanic |
| Lake | Landan | Lannie |
| Lakee | Landcaster | Lanning |
| Lakeisha | Landel | Lanny |
| Lakes | Lander | Lano |
| Lakesha | Landers | Lanphere |
| Lakeshia | Landes | Lanping |
| Lakey | Landi | Lanse |
| Lakeysha | Landick | Lansin |
| Lakin | Landis | Lansing |
| Lakisha | Lando | Lanstra |
| Lalonde | Landon | Lantz |
| Lam | Landowska | Lanway |
| Laman | Landram | Lanzer |
| Lamar | Landreth | Laparne |
| Lamaur | Landru | Lapriel |
| Lamb | Landrum | Laquita |
| Lambert | Lands | Lara |
| Lamesa | Lane | Larae |
| Lamont | Laneise | Larame |
| Lamora | Lanelle | Laramei |
| Lamour | Lanette | Larami |
| Lamphere | Lang | Laramie |
| Lamsek | Langdon | Lardee |
| Lamton | Lange | Lardel |
| Lamy | Langer | Lare |
| Lana | Langhoff | Laredo |
| Lanae | Langley | Lareer |
| Lanai | Langram | Larena |
| Lanark | Langrock | Laressa |
| Lancaster | Langton | Lariet |
| Lance | Langworth | Larissa |
| Lancelot | Lanh | Lark |

Larkin
Larnell
Laron
Larrabee
Larrinea
Larry
Lars
Larsen
Larson
Larue
Las Vegas
Laser
Lashanda
Lashawn
Lasher
Lashonda
Lasimha
Laslan
Lasley
Lassale
Lassen
Lassit
Lassiter
Last
Latah
Latakia
Latanya
Latasha
Latch
Late
Latenser
Later
Laterno
Lathrop

Latierno
Latin
Latisha
Latitude
Latonia
Latonya
Latosha
Latoshia
Latoya
Latreva
Latrice
Latricia
Lattie
Latty
Lau
Lauder
Laue
Laughlin
Laughter
Launa
Launceston
Launch
Laungayan
Launston
Launton
Laura
Laureen
Laurel
Lauren
Laurence
Laurens
Laurent
Lauretta
Laurette

Lauri
Laurie
Laurinda
Laurine
Lauris
Laurita
Lauryn
Lausanne
Lava
Lavada
Lavel
Lavelle
Lavendar
Lavender
Lavenia
Laver
Lavera
Lavern
Laverna
Laverne
Lavers
Lavina
Lavinia
Lavon
Lavonne
Lavra
Law
Lawanda
Lawerence
Lawert
Lawine
Lawler
Lawn
Lawr

Lawrence
Lawry
Lawson
Lawton
Layce
Layla
Layman
Laymon
Layne
Laysan
Layton
Laz
Lazar
Lazaro
Lazarus
Laze
Lazelle
Lazure
Le
Lea
Leach
Lead
Leaf
Leafy
Leah
Leak
Leal
Leamon
Leana
Leander
Leandra
Leann
Leanna
Leanne

Leary
Lease
Leatha
Leather
Leatherwood
Leatrice
Leave
Leaven
Leaver
Leavey
Leavon
Leavonworth
Lebanon
Lebaron
Lebec
Leben
Lebon
Leda
Ledden
Ledge
Ledger
Lee
Leeander
Leeann
Leed
Leege
Leeman
Leeroy
Leesa
Leffler
Lefler
Lefotu
Left
Leftie

Legend
Legg
Leggett
Legry
Leham
Lehman
Lei
Leia
Leif
Leigh
Leighenn
Leighton
Leila
Leilani
Lein
Leine
Leingang
Leinweber
Leisa
Leiseth
Leisha
Leiske
Leisure
Leitch
Leithold
Leitz
Lejeune
Lejon
Lek
Lekysha
Lela
Lelah
Leland
Lelia

Leman
Lemans
Lemanu
Lemar
Lemcke
Lemon
Lemonds
Lempi
Lemuel
Len
Lena
Lenah
Lenard
Lenberg
Lenette
Leng
Lenger
Lenhart
Leni
Lenihan
Lenius
Lenlie
Lenman
Lenna
Lennard
Lennette
Lennie
Lennier
Lennon
Lennox
Lenny
Leno
Lenora
Lenore

Lenox
Lensegrav
Lenssen
Lensy
Lenton
Lentz
Lenzi
Leo
Leola
Leon
Leona
Leonard
Leonardo
Leone
Leonel
Leonor
Leonora
Leonore
Leopard
Leopold
Leopoldo
Leoppard
Leora
Leota
Lera
Leric
Lerlin
Lerlina
Leroue
Leroy
Les
Lesa
Lesia
Lesich

Lesko
Leskovac
Lesley
Lesli
Leslie
Lesly
Lesman
Lesmeister
Leso
Lesser
Lessie
Lesson
Lester
Leta
Letah
Letal
Leth
Letha
Lethesa
Leticia
Letitia
Lett
Letter
Lettie
Letusha
Lev
Levar
Level
Levengood
Levey
Levi
Levie
Levka
Levon

| | | |
|---|---|---|
| Levvie | Liddell | Lily |
| Levy | Lidia | Lilyan |
| Lew | Lido | Lim |
| Lewellyn | Lidren | Limb |
| Lewin | Lids | Lime |
| Lewis | Liebman | Limit |
| Lex | Lief | Limotti |
| Lexi | Liem | Lin |
| Lexie | Lienne | Lina |
| Lexington | Life | Lincoln |
| Lexitte | Liffick | Lind |
| Lexus | Liga | Linda |
| Leyden | Light | Lindaas |
| Li | Lightening | Lindahl |
| Lia | Lighter | Lindal |
| Liable | Lihua | Lindaley |
| Liacia | Lihue | Lindberg |
| Liam | Like | Lindee |
| Lian | Likely | Lindell |
| Liana | Lila | Lindemann |
| Liance | Lile | Linden |
| Liane | Lilely | Linder |
| Lianna | Liles | Lindgren |
| Liarra | Liley | Lindquist |
| Libbie | Lilia | Lindsay |
| Libby | Lilian | Lindsey |
| Libert | Liliana | Lindskov |
| Libertine | Lilith | Lindsley |
| Liberty | Lilla | Lindy |
| Libra | Lilliam | Line |
| Libya | Lillian | Linea |
| License | Lillie | Linette |
| Licia | Lilly | Linger |
| Lida | Lilmousine | Linine |

| | | |
|---|---|---|
| Linn | Litch | Lloyd |
| Linnea | Litcha | Lmerline |
| Linnet | Liter | Loa |
| Linnie | Lithia | Loan |
| Linsay | Litia | Local |
| Linsey | Little | Locale |
| Linton | Littlefield | Locan |
| Lintow | Littleton | Lochan |
| Linville | Litton | Lochmann |
| Linwood | Liu | Lochmiller |
| Linz | Liufau | Lochran |
| Linza | Liuska | Lock |
| Linze | Liv | Locke |
| Linzey | Live | Lockes |
| Linzy | Lively | Lockhart |
| Lion | Livermore | Lockwood |
| Lionel | Livia | Lodeen |
| Liotti | Livingston | Loden |
| Lip | Livorno | Lodge |
| Lipid | Livvy | Lodger |
| Lisa | Lixi | Lodz |
| Lisbeth | Lixton | Loen |
| Lisco | Liya | Loescher |
| Lisel | Liz | Loew |
| Lisette | Liza | Loewecke |
| Lisha | Lizabeth | Lofgren |
| Lisimba | Lizbeth | Lofton |
| LiSimba | Lizeth | Log |
| Lisle | Lizette | Logan |
| Lissa | Lizton | Logsdon |
| Lissen | Lizzie | Logue |
| Lissette | Llano | Lohman |
| Listen | Llewellyn | Lois |
| Lister | Llinton | Loki |

| | | |
|---|---|---|
| Lokkan | Loraine | Lost |
| Lokken | Loran | Lot |
| Lola | Lorane | Lott |
| Lolita | Lorang | Lotte |
| Loma | Loranz | Lottery |
| Loman | Lorayne | Lottie |
| Lomas | Lord | Lotto |
| Lomm | Loredo | Lotus |
| Lon | Loree | Lou |
| Lona | Loren | Louann |
| Londborg | Lorena | Loucks |
| London | Lorene | Loud |
| Lone | Lorentson | Louella |
| Long | Lorenz | Lougheed |
| Longden | Lorenza | Louie |
| Longer | Lorenzo | Louis |
| Longfellow | Loretta | Louisa |
| Longine | Lori | Louise |
| Longitude | Loriann | Louisiana |
| Longton | Lorie | Loukanov |
| Longview | Lorin | Loukas |
| Longwith | Lorinda | Lounden |
| Loni | Lorine | Lourdes |
| Lonie | Lorissa | Louton |
| Lonnie | Lorizan | Louvenia |
| Lonny | Lorna | Louvon |
| Lonzo | Lorne | Love |
| Look | Lorraine | Lovena |
| Loomis | Lorrania | Lovett |
| Loper | Lorre | Lovey |
| Lopez | Lorri | Lovgren |
| Lopp | Lorrie | Lovick |
| Loque | Lorry | Lovie |
| Lora | Lorus | Loving |

| | | |
|---|---|---|
| Low | Lucienne | Luminia |
| Lowdes | Lucile | Lumsden |
| Lowe | Lucille | Lumunia |
| Lowell | Lucinda | Luna |
| Lowery | Lucius | Lunar |
| Lowrance | Luck | Lund |
| Lowri | Lucky | Lundeen |
| Lowrie | Lucretia | Lundin |
| Lowry | Lucy | Lundstrom |
| Loy | Ludden | Lunik |
| Loyal | Ludell | Luong |
| Loyce | Ludeman | Lupe |
| Loyd | Ludie | Lupo |
| Loyola | Ludwig | Lupone |
| Ltakia | Lue | Lupton |
| Luann | Luedeking | Luquecha |
| Luanne | Luella | Lur |
| Lubec | Luetta | Lura |
| Luca | Lufkin | Luri |
| Lucan | Lui | Lurissa |
| Lucas | Luicrezia | Lurline |
| Luccas | Luigi | Lusk |
| Luccio | Luis | Lusky |
| Luce | Luisa | Lute |
| Lucera | Luiten | Lutecha |
| Lucern | Luiza | Lutera |
| Lucerne | Luka | Luther |
| Lucero | Lukas | Lutz |
| Lucia | Luke | Lutzkanov |
| Lucian | Lukin | Luvenia |
| Lucianna | Lula | Lux |
| Luciano | Lulani | Luz |
| Lucie | Lumbago | Luzerne |
| Lucien | Lumini | Luzury |

| | | |
|---|---|---|
| L'Vonne | Lyn | Lynse |
| Lwin | Lynch | Lynsey |
| Ly | Lynda | Lynwood |
| Lyal | Lyndell | Lynx |
| Lyall | Lyndolyn | Lyon |
| Lyda | Lyndon | Lyons |
| Lydia | Lyndsay | Lyric |
| Lyen | Lyndsey | Lyricia |
| Lyette | Lynella | Lysa |
| Lyla | Lynette | Lysen |
| Lyle | Lynise | Lysle |
| Lyman | Lynn | Lyson |
| Lymic | Lynne | Lyster |
| Lympic | Lynnette | Lytsell |

M is for "Mothers" and the Miracle of birth
And the Magic in your name once you come to this earth.

| | | |
|---|---|---|
| Ma | Machelle | Maclaren |
| Maadaan | Machiko | Maclean |
| Maas | Machin | Macmaster |
| Mabbott | Machina | Macmilliam |
| Mabel | Macie | MacNealy |
| Mabelle | Macintire | MacNeil |
| Mable | Macintyre | Maco |
| Mabry | Mack | Macon |
| Mac | Mackay | Macro |
| Macadam | Macke | Macroberts |
| Macan | Mackenna | Macy |
| Macauley | MacKenzie | Madaline |
| Macclellan | Mackenzie | Madalyn |
| MacCormick | Mackey | Madam |
| Maccullough | Macki | Madan |
| Macdonald | Mackinley | Madden |
| Macdonnel | Mackinney | Maddie |
| Macdonnell | Mackintosh | Madding |
| Mace | Mackler | Maddison |
| Maceagan | Macklin | Maddock |
| Maceo | Maclain | Maddox |
| Macey | Maclaine | Madeleine |

| | | |
|---|---|---|
| Madeline | Magdalene | Maia |
| Madelyn | Magee | Maida |
| Maden | Magen | Maiden |
| Madera | Magenta | Maii |
| Madge | Maggee | Maile |
| Madie | Maggie | Main |
| Madisen | Maggy | Maine |
| Madison | Magiba | Mair |
| Madisyn | Magic | Maira |
| Madock | Magician | Maise |
| Madonna | Magnificent | Maisha |
| Mador | Magnolia | Maitilde |
| Madra | Magnoni | Maius |
| Madras | Magnum | Maiven |
| Madrid | Magnus | Maiz |
| Madris | Magnuson | Maize |
| Madrona | Maguire | Majerus |
| Madsen | Maha | Majic |
| Madsoen | Mahadev | Major |
| Madtson | Mahaffey | Mak |
| Mady | Mahala | Makah |
| Madysen | Mahalia | Makail |
| Mae | Mahamm | Makala |
| Maegan | Mahan | Makale |
| Maeli | Maher | Makana |
| Maelys | Mahir | Makara |
| Maesa | Mahlon | Makari |
| Maeve | Mahmood | Makayla |
| Maeven | Mahmoud | Makeba |
| Mafalda | Mahogany | Makenna |
| Maganoui | Mahon | Makenzie |
| Magart | Mahre | Makhlouf |
| Magdalen | Mahugh | Maki |
| Magdalena | Mai | Makin |

| | | |
|---|---|---|
| Makka | Mallow | Mango |
| Makos | Malloy | Manhattan |
| Maks | Malone | Manibusan |
| Maksem | Maloney | Manicke |
| Maksim | Maloy | Manila |
| Maksome | Malsch | Maniloe |
| Mala | Malt | Manilow |
| Malacca | Malta | Manis |
| Malachi | Maltos | Manke |
| Malachy | Malva | Mankus |
| Malakai | Malvesia | Manlae |
| Malawa | Malvina | Manley |
| Malaya | Mamie | Manlie |
| Malcolm | Mamlette | Manlow |
| Malcom | Mammie | Mann |
| Malde | Mamuye | Manner |
| Maldom | Man | Manning |
| Malena | Manassa | Mannis |
| Mali | Mancha | Mannix |
| Malia | Manchas | Mano |
| Malik | Manchester | Manor |
| Malin | Mandan | Manouchehr |
| Malina | Mandate | Mansfield |
| Malinda | Mandela | Mansfile |
| Malise | Mandell | Mansion |
| Malissa | Mandi | Manson |
| Malkam | Mandie | Mansour |
| Mallahan | Mandrell | Manthey |
| Malleck | Mandy | Mantos |
| Mallen | Mane | Manuel |
| Mallie | Manee | Manuela |
| Mallone | Manenica | Manus |
| Mallor | Manford | Mao |
| Mallory | Mangaliman | Map |

| | | |
|---|---|---|
| Mapanao | Mardy | Maribel |
| Maples | Marea | Maribeth |
| Mara | Marek | Maricela |
| Marakei | Maren | Marie |
| Maralyn | Margan | Mariel |
| Maranda | Marganelli | Mariela |
| Marathon | Margaret | Mariet |
| Marathone | Margarete | Marietta |
| Marbut | Margarett | Marigold |
| Marc | Margaretta | Mariko |
| Marca | Margarette | Marilee |
| Marcel | Margarita | Marilyn |
| Marcela | Margarito | Marilynn |
| Marcelina | Margaux | Mariman |
| Marceline | Marge | Marina |
| Marcelino | Margery | Marini |
| Marcella | Margie | Marinig |
| Marcelle | Margit | Marino |
| Marcellus | Margo | Mario |
| Marcelo | Margot | Marion |
| March | Margret | Maris |
| Marchant | Margreta | Marisa |
| Marchelle | Marguerite | Marisela |
| Marchial | Mari | Marisol |
| Marchland | Maria | Marissa |
| Marci | Mariah | Maristella |
| Marcia | Mariam | Maritza |
| Marcie | Marian | Marivic |
| Marcile | Mariana | Marj |
| Marcille | Mariane | Marjorie |
| Marco | Mariann | Marjory |
| Marcos | Marianna | Mark |
| Marcus | Marianne | Marked |
| Marcy | Mariano | Market |

| | | |
|---|---|---|
| Markette | Marq | Marvel |
| Markham | Marquardt | Marvin |
| Marki | Marque | Marx |
| Markku | Marques | Mary |
| Markus | Marquette | Marya |
| Markuson | Marquez | Maryah |
| Marla | Marquis | Maryal |
| Marlboro | Marquise | Maryann |
| Marlborough | Marquiss | Maryanne |
| Marlburo | Marquita | Marybelle |
| Marle | Marr | Marybeth |
| Marlean | Marrah | Maryellen |
| Marlee | Marriott | Mary-Helen |
| Marlena | Marrolf | Maryhill |
| Marlene | Marry | Maryjane |
| Marlesa | Mars | Maryjo |
| Marletta | Marsh | Maryland |
| Marley | Marsha | Marylin |
| Marlie | Marshall | Marylou |
| Marlin | Marshelle | Marysa |
| Marlise | Marston | Maryse |
| Marlo | Marta | Marysia |
| Marlon | Martha | Maryzulil |
| Marlow | Marti | Marz |
| Marlys | Martin | Marzia |
| Marlyta | Martina | Masa |
| Marmalade | Martine | Masha |
| Marmalaid | Martiner | Masina |
| Marney | Martinez | Mask |
| Marnie | Martini | Maskell |
| Maro | Martinson | Mason |
| Maroa | Marty | Masoud |
| Marona | Martz | Massachusetts |
| Maroon | Marva | Massie |

| | | |
|---|---|---|
| Masten | Mattison | Mawena |
| Mastin | Mattler | Max |
| Mat | Mattson | Maxamus |
| Mata | Mattus | Maxen |
| Match | Matty | Maxey |
| Matelda | Matzelle | Maxha |
| Matelle | Maud | Maxi |
| Mateo | Mauddie | Maxie |
| Mathena | Maude | Maxik |
| Mathew | Maudie | Maxime |
| Mathews | Maudina | Maximilian |
| Mathias | Maudlin | Maximillia |
| Mathilda | Mauerman | Maximino |
| Mathilde | Maul | Maximo |
| Mathis | Maupin | Maximus |
| Mathisen | Maura | Maxine |
| Mathison | Maureen | Maxton |
| Matilda | Maurene | Maxwell |
| Matilde | Maurer | Maxy |
| Matison | Maurette | May |
| Matlick | Mauriac | May Lisa |
| Matlock | Maurice | Maya |
| Matrix | Mauricio | Mayahara |
| Mats | Maurine | Mayala |
| Matso | Mauritania | Mayan |
| Matson | Mauritus | Maybee |
| Matt | Maurizia | Maybell |
| Matteo | Maurret | Maybelle |
| Matteson | Maury | Maye |
| Matthew | Maurya | Mayer |
| Matthews | Maverick | Mayfield |
| Matti | Mavis | Mayhew |
| Mattice | Maw | Mayme |
| Mattie | Mawdsley | Maymie |

| | | |
|---|---|---|
| Maynard | McCarthy | McDole |
| Mayoh | McCartney | McDonald |
| Mayor | McCastlin | McDonald |
| Mayotte | McCaw | McDonnel |
| Mayra | McClain | McDougal |
| Maytie | McClanahan | McDougul |
| Mayton | McClary | McDowell |
| Maza | McClasin | McDuffie |
| Mazatlan | McClintick | McDuffy |
| Mazda | McClosky | McFadden |
| Maze | McClould | McFarland |
| Mazen | McClully | McGarrah |
| Mazi | McClure | McGill |
| Mazie | McCollum | McGinnis |
| Mazikowski | McConnaghy | McGiver |
| Mazoa | McConnon | McGourin |
| Mazon | McCool | McGowan |
| Mbuthia | McCord | McGraw |
| Mcabee | McCorkel | McGreen |
| McAbee | McCormack | McGuine |
| McAdams | McCormick | McGuire |
| McAfee | McCory | McGuirk |
| McAftery | McCowan | McHatton |
| M'Callaster | McCoy | McHough |
| McAllifee | McCracken | McHugh |
| McBe | McCrary | McIntire |
| McBride | McCrea | McIntosh |
| McCabe | McCreery | McKail |
| McCaffery | McCullogh | Mckayla |
| McCall | McCullough | McKeag |
| McCallaster | McCurdy | McKeal |
| McCallum | McDade | McKean |
| McCammon | McDaniel | McKee |
| McCarthney | McDermott | McKeegary |

| | | |
|---|---|---|
| McKeil | McPhal | Mechelle |
| McKelvy | McPhearson | Meda |
| McKenna | McPhike | Medack |
| McKenzie | McQueary | Medak |
| McKeon | McRae | Medal |
| McKernan | McRenolds | Medeco |
| McKinley | McTavish | Medha |
| McKinney | McVeigh | Medicine |
| McKinnie | McVey | Medina |
| McKinzie | Me | Medium |
| McKouwn | Mea | Medley |
| McLaine | Meacham | Medrano |
| McLane | Meade | Mee |
| McLaughlin | Meadoe | Meek |
| McLean | Meadow | Meeks |
| McLeod | Meadown | Meg |
| McMahan | Meadows | Mega |
| McMahon | Meagan | Megan |
| McManus | Meaghan | Meggi |
| McMasher | Meagher | Meghan |
| McMaster | Meagon | Meghann |
| McMillian | Meale | Meghla |
| McMorris | Meami | Mehetabel |
| McMullen | Means | Mehitabel |
| McMullin | Meara | Mehrdad |
| McMurry | Mearl | Mehring |
| McNabb | Mearr | Mehrsadeh |
| McNally | Measure | Meinzer |
| McNamara | Meave | Meischke |
| McNeal | Meaven | Meister |
| McNealy | Mec | Meka |
| McNeil | Mecaha | Mekka |
| McNeilly | Mecca | Mel |
| McNutt | Mechell | Melain |

| | | |
|---|---|---|
| Melaina | Mellon | Menolly |
| Melaine | Melloney | Mentasta |
| Melani | Mellow | Mentos |
| Melania | Melly | Menzia |
| Melanie | Melnick | Merae |
| Melany | Melodee | Meranda |
| Melba | Melodie | Merc |
| Melbourne | Melody | Mercado |
| Melby | Meloe | Merce |
| Melessa | Melon | Mercedalia |
| Meli | Melonie | Mercedas |
| Melia | Melony | Mercedes |
| Melice | Melosa | Mercer |
| Melicent | Meloso | Mercia |
| Melina | Meloy | Mercida |
| Melinda | Melso | Mercredi |
| Melis | Melton | Mercury |
| Melisa | Melusine | Mercy |
| Melisande | Melva | Merdi |
| Melise | Melville | Meredee |
| Melisenda | Melvin | Meredeth |
| Melisendra | Melvina | Meredith |
| Meliss | Melynda | Meri |
| Melissa | Member | Merial |
| Melisse | Memez | Meridian |
| Melita | Memorial | Meridith |
| Mellen | Memory | Meriel |
| Melleta | Memphis | Merifield |
| Mellicent | Menas | Merilee |
| Mellie | Mendenhall | Merilla |
| Mellisa | Mendocino | Merino |
| Mellissa | Mendon | Meris |
| Mellita | Mendoza | Merissa |
| Mellody | Menefee | Merit |

| | | |
|---|---|---|
| Merkel | Mesich | Michaelson |
| Merl | Message | Michaila |
| Merl | Messay | Michalak |
| Merla | Messick | Michale |
| Merle | Messina | Michaliszyn |
| Merlin | Messmer | Micheal |
| Merlyn | Meta | Michel |
| Merna | Metal | Michelangelo |
| Meroe | Metcalf | Michele |
| Merola | Meteor | Michelina |
| Merri | Meter | Micheline |
| Merrick | Methqal | Michell |
| Merrie | Methusela | Michelle |
| Merrielle | Metro | Michelsen |
| Merril | Metrokas | Michigan |
| Merrill | Mettler | Mickel |
| Merriot | Metzler | Mickey |
| Merritt | Meyer | Micki |
| Merry | Meyers | Mickie |
| Merryman | Mia | Micky |
| Mershon | Miaka | Micro |
| Merth | Miami | Middle |
| Mertice | Miara | Middleton |
| Mertie | Miata | Midge |
| Mertle | Mica | Midkiff |
| Merton | Micaela | Midland |
| Mertz | Micah | Midler |
| Merula | Mich | Midnight |
| Mervin | Michael | Mielke |
| Merwyn | Michaela | Miernyk |
| Meryl | Michaele | Migdalia |
| Merzario | Michaelina | Mighty |
| Mesa | Michaeline | Miglia |
| Meschach | Michaella | Mignon |

| | | |
|---|---|---|
| Mignonette | Milford | Minchen |
| Miguel | Milicent | Mind |
| Miguela | Miliscent | Mindi |
| Migueli | Milise | Mindy |
| Miguelita | Milissent | Mine |
| Mika | Milka | Miner |
| Mikaela | Milklos | Minerich |
| Mikala | Mill | Minerva |
| Mikasa | Milla | Minette |
| Mikayla | Millar | Mini |
| Mike | Millard | Minion |
| Mikel | Milleah | Mink |
| Mikelina | Miller | Minna |
| Mikelsen | Millersylvania | Minnelli |
| Mikenzie | Milli | Minnesota |
| Mikesell | Milliani | Minnick |
| Mikhail | Millicent | Minnie |
| Miki | Millie | Minns |
| Mikkelsen | Million | Minny |
| Mikko | Millones | Minolta |
| Mikolas | Mills | Minor |
| Mil | Milly | Minten |
| Mila | Milo | Minuette |
| Milagros | Milor | Minute |
| Milala | Miloscia | Minx |
| Milan | Milton | Miquel |
| Milari | Milyscent | Mir |
| Milburn | Milzie | Mira |
| Mildred | Mim | Miracle |
| Mildrid | Mimi | Miranda |
| Mile | Mimieux | Mire |
| Milena | Mimosa | Mirek |
| Miler | Min | Mirella |
| Miles | Mina | Mirelle |

| | | |
|---|---|---|
| Mires | Mitchell | Mohammed |
| Mireya | Mitford | Mohar |
| Miria | Mittie | Mohney |
| Miriam | Mitzi | Moina |
| Mirilla | Mix | Moini |
| Mirna | Mixe | Moira |
| Mironon | Mixie | Moire |
| Miroton | Mixon | Moireach |
| Mirra | Mize | Moises |
| Mirror | Mizuhata | Moishe |
| Mirtle | Mizuta | Molash |
| Misa | M'liss | Mold |
| Misael | Moatazedian | Molene |
| Misako | Moberg | Molina |
| Misato | Moberly | Moline |
| Mischa | Mobile | Moll |
| Mischell | Mock | Mollen |
| Mishayla | Moco | Mollie |
| Misiak | Modena | Molly |
| Misiasz | Modesta | Molohon |
| Misitano | Modesto | Molokai |
| Miso | Modesty | Moloney |
| Missia | Modica | Moltz |
| Missie | Moe | Molyneux |
| Mission | Moeller | Momeni |
| Mississippi | Moen | Mona |
| Missouri | Moergen | Monaco |
| Missy | Moffitt | Monahan |
| Mist | Mohab | Monca |
| Misti | Mohamad | Monday |
| Mistic | Mohamed | Monette |
| Misty | Mohamedali | Monfe |
| Mitch | Mohammad | Monica |
| Mitchel | Mohammadi | Monika |

| | | |
|---|---|---|
| Monillas | Moored | Morishige |
| Monion | Moorehead | Moritz |
| Monique | Moores | Morley |
| Monna | Moorhead | Morna |
| Monnin | Moorman | Mornay |
| Monnrise | Moose | Morning |
| Monroe | Mopsy | Morningstar |
| Monrovia | Moq | Morocco |
| Mons | Mora | Morraco |
| Monsanto | Morace | Morran |
| Monserrate | Morae | Morrell |
| Monsey | Morag | Morrill |
| Monson | Moran | Morris |
| Monsoon | Morava | Morrison |
| Monstar | Morby | Morrow |
| Montana | Mordred | Morse |
| Monte | More | Mortal |
| Montecarlo | Morea | Mortensen |
| Monterey | Moreau | Morteza |
| Montesano | Moreen | Mortimer |
| Montgelas | Morehead | Morton |
| Montgomery | Morehouse | Mosby |
| Montoya | Moreland | Mose |
| Montreal | Morena | Mosen |
| Monty | Morenci | Moses |
| Moody | Moreno | Moshe |
| Moomaw | Moretta | Mosheh |
| Moon | Morey | Moskal |
| Moonbeam | Morgan | Moss |
| Mooney | Morgana | Mossie |
| Moonstar | Morgenstern | Mosstafa |
| Moonunit | Moria | Most |
| Moor | Moriah | Mostaghimi |
| Moore | Morin | Mostowfy |

| | | |
|---|---|---|
| Mota | Muchoney | Murdock |
| Motes | Mucken | Murial |
| Mothra | Muddy | Muriel |
| Motion | Muehlbauer | Murielle |
| Motor | Mueille | Murison |
| Motoyoshi | Mueller | Murita |
| Motzer | Muffie | Murl |
| Mounaier | Muffler | Murphey |
| Mount | Muhammad | Murphy |
| Mountain | Muire | Murray |
| Mounts | Muireall | Murrell |
| Mouse | Muirgheal | Murren |
| Mousse | Mukhtar | Murry |
| Mouton | Mukilteo | Murshed |
| Movie | Mulberry | Muse |
| Mowlda | Mulhern | Music |
| Mowlds | Muligan | Musical |
| Mowo | Mullen | Mussel |
| Mowry | Mulliken | Mustafa |
| Mox | Mullin | Mustang |
| Moxcey | Mumma | Mutetelia |
| Moxie | Munawar | Mutton |
| Moxley | Muncy | Mutual |
| Moxy | Munday | My |
| Moya | Munich | Mya |
| Moyer | Munindra | Myah |
| Moylan | Munns | Mychal |
| Moyna | Munro | Myer |
| Moyra | Munsey | Myers |
| Mozambique | Munsinger | Myhr |
| Mozell | Munson | Myhres |
| Mozella | Munzi | Myint |
| Mozelle | Muphy | Mykra |
| Much | Muraglia | Mylanta |

| Myles | Myrilla | Myrtice |
| Mylos | Myrl | Myrtie |
| Myly | Myrle | Myrtis |
| Mynah | Myrlene | Myrtle |
| Mynt | Myrna | Mysorski |
| Myra | Myron | Mystery |
| Myranda | Myrrh | Mystic |
| Myria | Myrt | Mystical |
| Myriam | Myrta | Mystik |
| Myrige | Myrtia | Myth |

N is for "Nurturing" that I'll do through your years
to cuddle and comfort and calm all your fears.

| | | |
|---|---|---|
| Nabaie | Nakia | Nannery |
| Nabil | Nakima | Nannette |
| Nabors | Nakina | Nanney |
| Nacario | Nakola | Nanni |
| Naciemento | Nall | Nannie |
| Nacimento | Nallen | Nanny |
| Naco | Namaho | Nanon |
| Nada | Namet | Nansie |
| Nadara | Namiranian | Nanton |
| Nadezhda | Nan | Nanty |
| Nadia | Nana | Naoma |
| Nadine | Nance | Naomi |
| Nafisa | Nanci | Napel |
| Nagel | Nancie | Naples |
| Nagy | Nancsie | Napoleon |
| Nai | Nancy | Napoli |
| Naiad | Nanda | Narciso |
| Nail | Nandor | Narine |
| Naimabadi | Nanette | Narramore |
| Nairobi | Nani | Narrance |
| Najee | Nanita | Narrow |
| Nake | Nanna | Narrows |

| | | |
|---|---|---|
| Nash | Natosha | Nebiyou |
| Nasha | Natty | Nebraska |
| Nashe | Natural | Nebula |
| Nashville | Nature | Necro |
| Nasie | Natya | Ned |
| Nason | Nau | Neda |
| Nassau | Naught | Nedda |
| Nastalya | Nault | Nedi |
| Nastasia | Nauman | Nedira |
| Nastassia | Naut | Nediva |
| Nastassie | Nautical | Nedjelja |
| Nastassja | Navagate | Nedra |
| Nastenka | Navaho | Nedrow |
| Nat | Navales | Nee |
| Natala | Navarro | Neecia |
| Natalia | Navel | Needham |
| Natalie | Navickis | Neek |
| Nataline | Navigate | Neel |
| Natalis | Navigator | Neeley |
| Nataly | Navin | Neelin |
| Natasha | Navy | Neely |
| Natashia | Naximento | Neema |
| Nate | Nayeli | Neff |
| Nathalia | Naylor | Neher |
| Nathalie | Naziemento | Neil |
| Nathan | Nazimento | Neiland |
| Nathanael | Nazir | Neill |
| Nathanial | Nduta | Neilsen |
| Nathaniel | Nea | Neilson |
| Natili | Neah | Neilton |
| Nation | Neal | Neimi |
| Native | Nearing | Neisinger |
| Natividad | Nebbitt | Nekia |
| Naton | Nebergall | Nekoda |

| | | |
|---|---|---|
| Nela | Nessi | Newell |
| Nelanie | Nessie | Newett |
| Nelda | Nessy | Newhampshire |
| Nelia | Nesta | Newhaven |
| Nelie | Nestor | Newhouse |
| Nelina | Neta | Newlean |
| Nelita | Netta | Newlun |
| Nell | Nettie | Newman |
| Nella | Netty | Newport |
| Nelle | Neubert | News |
| Nellette | Neuenschwander | Newsey |
| Nellianna | Neuert | Newsom |
| Nellie | Neufeldt | Newton |
| Nelly | Neuman | Ney |
| Nels | Neva | Neylon |
| Nelsen | Nevada | Neysa |
| Nelson | Nevaeh | Nezika |
| Nendell | Neve | Ng |
| Nenzel | Never | Ngoc |
| Neo | Neve'r | Nguyen |
| Neodisha | Nevil | Ngy |
| Neola | Nevin | Nia |
| Neoma | Nevitt | Niagara |
| Neon | Nevsa | Niah |
| Nepal | New | Niana |
| Nepalese | New Jersey | Niara |
| Neptune | New Mexico | Nicaela |
| Nereida | New York | Nice |
| Nereo | Newarch | Nichol |
| Nergan | Newark | Nichola |
| Nero | Newberry | Nicholas |
| Nesmith | Newboles | Nicholaus |
| Ness | Newbury | Nichole |
| Nessa | Newcomb | Nichols |

| | | |
|---|---|---|
| Nicholson | Nikhil | Niquette |
| Nicia | Niki | Nisbet |
| Nick | Nikita | Nisco |
| Nickel | Nikki | Nissan |
| Nickell | Niklas | Nissell |
| Nicki | Nikle | Nissen |
| Nickie | Niko | Nita |
| Nicklaus | Nikol | Nitchman |
| Nickolas | Nikolai | Nixanne |
| Nickole | Nikolas | Nixian |
| Nickson | Nikole | Nixie |
| Nicky | Nikon | Nixion |
| Nico | Nikos | Nixon |
| Nicol | Nila | Nizhone |
| Nicola | Niland | Nnambi |
| Nicolas | Nilda | Noa |
| Nicole | Nile | Noah |
| Nicolette | Niles | Noam |
| Nicolina | Nils | Noaz |
| Nicoline | Nilsa | Nobility |
| Nicolle | Nilsen | Noble |
| Niconina | Nilson | Noclo |
| Niday | Nilsson | Nocol |
| Nielsen | Nima | Noe |
| Nielson | Nimbus | Noel |
| Niemela | Nimo | Noella |
| Niemi | Nin | Noelle |
| Nieves | Nina | Noemi |
| Nigel | Ninetta | Noine |
| Night | Ninette | Nola |
| Nihau | Ninia | Nolan |
| Nihipali | Ninnette | Noland |
| Nika | Nino | Nolie |
| Nike | Ninon | Noll |

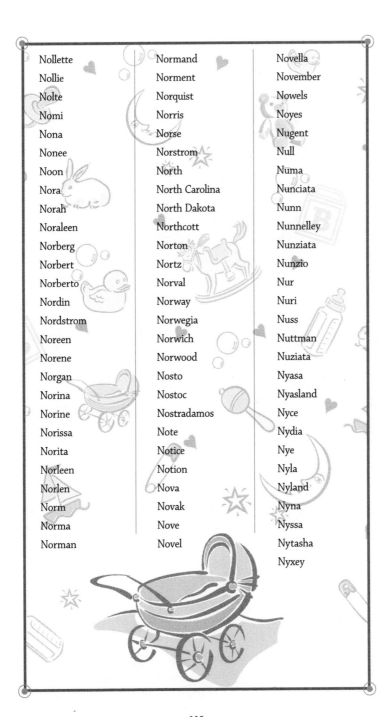

| | | |
|---|---|---|
| Nollette | Normand | Novella |
| Nollie | Norment | November |
| Nolte | Norquist | Nowels |
| Nomi | Norris | Noyes |
| Nona | Norse | Nugent |
| Nonee | Norstrom | Null |
| Noon | North | Numa |
| Nora | North Carolina | Nunciata |
| Norah | North Dakota | Nunn |
| Noraleen | Northcott | Nunnelley |
| Norberg | Norton | Nunziata |
| Norbert | Nortz | Nunzio |
| Norberto | Norval | Nur |
| Nordin | Norway | Nuri |
| Nordstrom | Norwegia | Nuss |
| Noreen | Norwich | Nuttman |
| Norene | Norwood | Nuziata |
| Norgan | Nosto | Nyasa |
| Norina | Nostoc | Nyasland |
| Norine | Nostradamos | Nyce |
| Norissa | Note | Nydia |
| Norita | Notice | Nye |
| Norleen | Notion | Nyla |
| Norlen | Nova | Nyland |
| Norm | Novak | Nyna |
| Norma | Nove | Nyssa |
| Norman | Novel | Nytasha |
| | | Nyxey |

O is for "Openness" that I hope that we'll share.
To always be close, confide and care.

| | | |
|---|---|---|
| O'Connor | Oceanus | Odis |
| O'Leary | Ocena | Oditz |
| Oak | Ocho | Odom |
| Oakley | Ochs | Odysseus |
| Oasis | Ocie | Odyssey |
| Obadiah | Ocobock | Oenning |
| Obedience | O'Connor | Oestreich |
| Obedient | Octave | Ofdenkamp |
| Oberg | Octavia | Ofelia |
| Oberon | Octavie | Offenbach |
| Obi | Octavio | Ofilia |
| Obie | Octavion | Ogden |
| Obrian | October | Ogle |
| Obrien | Oda | O'Grady |
| O'Brien | Odealia | Oh |
| Obsessa | Odelia | Ohagan |
| Ocasta | Odell | O'Hara |
| Ocean | Odenrider | Ohio |
| Oceana | Odessa | Ohlson |
| Oceania | Odie | Ohm |
| Oceanna | Odilia | Oil |
| Oceansong | Odin | Oilton |

Ojo
Okamoto
Okanogan
Okaska
Okay
Oke
O'Keefe
Okey
Okihara
Oklahoma
Oknoten
Okoye
Ola
Olaf
Olallie
Olan
Olden
Olds
Ole
Olea
Oleg
Olen
Olena
Olene
Olenka
Olesh
Oleta
Olga
Olia
Oliance
Olibia
Olibuel
Olicia
Olimpia

Olin
Oline
Olinka
Oliva
Olivas
Olive
Oliver
Olivette
Olivetti
Olivia
Olk
Ollie
Olling
Ollivier
Olly
Olmstead
Olmsted
Olof
Olsen
Olson
Olton
Olva
Olympe
Olympia
Olympie
Olympius
Om
Oma
Omada
Omak
Oman
Omar
Omari
Omayra

Omega
Omer
Omoo
Ona
Onagain
Onali
Ondine
Ondra
Ondro
One
Oneal
Oneil
Oneill
Ong
Oni
Onie
O'Niel
Onkel
Onley
Only
Onna
Ono
Onomatopoeia
Onset
Onslow
Ontario
Onus
Oona
Opal
Opaline
Opcit
Opel
Opella
Open

| | | |
|---|---|---|
| Opey | Oriana | Ortensia |
| Opheim | Oriane | Ortiz |
| Ophelia | Orianna | Orval |
| Ophelie | Orie | Orvil |
| Ophira | Oriel | Orville |
| Ophis | Orien | Orwig |
| Opie | Oriene | O'Ryan |
| Oprah | Orient | Osama |
| Option | Oriette | Osborn |
| Ora | Orin | Osborne |
| Oral | Oriol | Osburn |
| Oralia | Oriole | Oscar |
| Oram | Orion | Oscarson |
| Oran | Orka | Osh |
| Orana | Orkas | O'Shay |
| Orange | Orlan | Oshel |
| Orbe | Orland | Oshkosh |
| Orca | Orlando | Oshton |
| Orcas | Orlena | Osilla |
| Orchard | Orlens | Osina |
| Orchid | Orlo | Osiris |
| Orcutt | Orlon | Oskar |
| Oree | Orlsel | Osmak |
| Oregon | Ormiston | Osmonovich |
| O'Reilly | Orourke | Osoyoos |
| O'Reily | Orpha | Ossie |
| Orel | Orr | Ossin |
| Orelee | Orren | Osterhout |
| Orelia | Orrico | Ostfeld |
| Oren | Orrin | Ostrom |
| Orena | Orsa | Osvaldo |
| Organa | Orsel | Oswald |
| Organza | Orseline | Otha |
| O'Rhyly | Ortas | Otho |

| | | |
|---|---|---|
| Otilia | Ottomatt | Owain |
| Otis | Oty | Oweis |
| Ott | Ouida | Owen |
| Ottavia | Ousley | Owens |
| Ottawa | Ova | Owings |
| Ottie | Ovalo | Oxford |
| Ottilie | Ovando | Oz |
| Ottis | Overland | Ozella |
| Otto | Overton | Ozone |
| Ottoman | Ovidiu | Ozzie |

P is for "Parents," Lord guide us, I pray.
For patience and wisdom to get through each day.

| | | |
|---|---|---|
| Pablo | Paiton | Pamelee |
| Pace | Pak | Pamelina |
| Pacheco | Paki | Pamella |
| Pacific | Palace | Pamlasue |
| Pacifica | Paladin | Pamlico |
| Pacifico | Palazzo | Pammie |
| Pack | Palisoc | Pammy |
| Packard | Palkovich | Pamper |
| Packer | Pallas | Pan |
| Padan | Palm | Panam |
| Paddan | Palma | Panama |
| Paddette | Palmen | Panamia |
| Pae | Palmer | Panamint |
| Page | Palo | Pananean |
| Pageanne | Paloma | Panda |
| Pager | Palomino | Pandora |
| Paige | Palouse | Pandoura |
| Painter | Pam | Pani |
| Paire | Pamala | Panis |
| Paise | Pamalee | Pannkuk |
| Paisey | Pamaliegh | Pansy |
| Paisley | Pamela | Pantor |

| | | |
|---|---|---|
| Paola | Parsons | Patrice |
| Paoletta | Part | Patricia |
| Paolina | Particia | Patrick |
| Paoline | Partin | Patrisha |
| Papac | Partisan | Patrizia |
| Paper | Partner | Patsy |
| Parade | Parton | Pattern |
| Paradis | Partridge | Patterson |
| Paradise | Parttan | Patti |
| Paramont | Pasco | Pattie |
| Pardini | Pascoe | Patton |
| Paretshi | Pascual | Patty |
| Parfinski | Paseo | Paul |
| Paris | Paso | Paula |
| Parise | Pasquale | Paule |
| Parison | Pass | Paulette |
| Park | Passage | Pauley |
| Parke | Passion | Paulina |
| Parker | Pasta | Pauline |
| Parking | Pastel | Paulinta |
| Parkinson | Pastoral | Paulit |
| Parklette | Pastrana | Paull |
| Parkmont | Pat | Pauly |
| Parkroyal | Patburg | Pave |
| Parks | Pate | Pavel |
| Parlari | Pateizia | Paver |
| Parnell | Patent | Pavia |
| Parns | Paterson | Pavlicek |
| Parriott | Path | Pawelka |
| Parrish | Pathe | Pawnee |
| Parry | Patience | Pawtucket |
| Parsell | Paton | Paxon |
| Parshotam | Patreyce | Paxson |
| Parson | Patrica | Paxton |

| | | |
|---|---|---|
| Pay | Pehl | Perch |
| Payne | Pela | Percival |
| Pays | Pelen | Percy |
| Payson | Peltier | Perez |
| Payton | Pemmican | Peri |
| Paz | Pen | Perigo |
| Peabody | Pena | Periwinkle |
| Peace | Pence | Perkins |
| Peaceful | Pend | Perla |
| Peach | Penelopa | Perle |
| Peaches | Penelope | Perna |
| Peak | Penilope | Pernell |
| Peake | Penina | Perpetua |
| Peal | Penine | Perquita |
| Pear | Penn | Perri |
| Pearcy | Penni | Perria |
| Pearl | Pennie | Perrine |
| Pearla | Penninsula | Perron |
| Pearle | Pennsylvania | Perry |
| Pearlie | Penny | Perse |
| Pearline | Penrose | Pershing |
| Pearsal | Pensee | Persia |
| Pearson | Penske | Person |
| Peck | Penta | Persy |
| Pedersen | People | Perth |
| Pedigo | Pepita | Perthy |
| Pedro | Pepito | Peru |
| Peek | Peppar | Peshastin |
| Peel | Pepper | Peshtaz |
| Peewee | Peppers | Pet |
| Peg | Peppery | Peta |
| Pegasus | Pepsi | Petal |
| Peggie | Per | Pete |
| Peggy | Peralta | Petek |

| | | |
|---|---|---|
| Peter | Philippa | Pick |
| Peterman | Philippine | Pickering |
| Peters | Philis | Pier |
| Petersen | Philla | Pierce |
| Peterson | Phillip | Piercie |
| Petit | Phillips | Pierpoint |
| Petra | Phillis | Pierre |
| Petrich | Philomena | Pierson |
| Petronella | Philpott | Piet |
| Petrozzi | Phineas | Pietro |
| Petterson | Phinnaeus | Pietz |
| Pettiford | Phinney | Piffle |
| Pettis | Phipps | Pigeon |
| Pettit | Phligh | Piggey |
| Petty | Phoebe | Pigion |
| Petula | Phoebus | Pike |
| Petulia | Phoenix | Pikka |
| Peugeot | Phoibe | Pilar |
| Peveril | Phone | Pilot |
| Peyton | Phonetta | Pilsner |
| Pfaff | Phono | Pilston |
| Pfitzer | Photo | Pimblico |
| Phaedra | Phrania | Pimento |
| Phaidra | Phullis | Pimlico |
| Pham | Phylicia | Pin |
| Phan | Phylida | Pine |
| Phanessa | Phylis | Pinelopie |
| Pheany | Phyllis | Pines |
| Phebe | Phyllys | Ping |
| Phelix | Pia | Pink |
| Phelps | Piaza | Pinkie |
| Phil | Picabo | Pinnacle |
| Philip | Picard | Pinnacles |
| Philipp | Picasso | Pinson |

| | | |
|---|---|---|
| Pip | Plotzki | Pont |
| Pipe | Plum | Ponte |
| Piper | Plumb | Ponter |
| Pippa | Plummer | Pontiac |
| Piroska | Pluto | Pontius |
| Piset | Plyllis | Pookie |
| Pismo | Plymouth | Poole |
| Pistil | Poe | Pope |
| Pitch | Poem | Poppy |
| Pitcher | Poenitsch | Poraj |
| Pittenger | Poers | Porcius |
| Pitts | Poet | Porfirio |
| Pixie | Poinsette | Porridge |
| Pixlee | Point | Porsche |
| Pixy | Pointer | Porsha |
| Pizazz | Poirier | Port |
| Place | Polar | Porte |
| Plae | Polda | Portello |
| Plaggerman | Poldervart | Porter |
| Plague | Pole | Portia |
| Plain | Policy | Portland |
| Plains | Polina | Posner |
| Plateau | Poll | Post |
| Plath | Pollari | Potomac |
| Platinum | Pollen | Potpourri |
| Plato | Pollock | Potts |
| Plaza | Polly | Poulsen |
| Pleasant | Pollyanna | Powder |
| Please | Polo | Powdery |
| Plenty | Polson | Powe |
| Plesha | Pompei | Powell |
| Plethora | Pompey | Power |
| Plichta | Pond | Powers |
| Plocki | Poni | Pownall |

Poythress

Prado

Prairie

Praise

Pratt

Prayer

Precious

Preedy

Preist

Prentice

Prentiss

Prescott

Presence

Present

Presler

Presley

Press

Presta

Prestige

Presto

Preston

Prestrud

Preuschoff

Price

Pricer

Pries

Priest

Priestess

Prieto

Prill

Primrose

Prince

Princess

Principal

Print

Printer

Prints

Pris

Priscilla

Priscus

Prism

Prissie

Pritchard

Pritchett

Private

Probart

Prochazka

Proctor

Proffitt

Profit

Promise

Propero

Prophet

Prospect

Prosperity

Prospero

Prosser

Prothero

Providence

Providenci

Provo

Proxi

Pru

Prudence

Prudente

Prudentia

Prudential

Prudhomme

Prudy

Prue

Pruitt

Pry

Psyche

Puerto Rico

Puffin

Pulita

Pulse

Pura

Pure

Puritania

Purity

Purple

Purser

Puterbaugh

Putman

Putscher

Putter

Pyeatt

Pyle

Pyramid

Pyrania

Pyrhette

Pyrmad

Pyro

Q is for "Questions" you'll ask at age three.
By then we'll be crazy, your father and me.

| | | |
|---|---|---|
| Qabil | Queene | Quillermo |
| Qake | Queener | Quimbey |
| Qasim | Queenie | Quimby |
| Quaid | Queens | Quinalt |
| Quaintance | Queisha | Quinault |
| Quake | Quench | Quince |
| Quaker | Quenna | Quincy |
| Quall | Quentilla | Quiney |
| Qualley | Quentin | Quinlan |
| Quan | Querida | Quinn |
| Quang | Quest | Quinna |
| Quant | Qu'Est | Quint |
| Quantas | Questi | Quintana |
| Quantrille | Question | Quintara |
| Quantum | Queue | Quinteiro |
| Quarry | Quiana | Quinten |
| Quartz | Quick | Quintin |
| Quay | Quidad | Quintina |
| Quaye | Quiet | Quinton |
| Que | Quigg | Quintos |
| Quebec | Quiggley | Quirin |
| Queen | Quill | Quita |
| Queena | Quillen | Quits |

146

R is for "Remarkable," that's what you are.
Your spirit is as bright as a shining star!

| | | |
|---|---|---|
| Rabekka | Radames | Rafaela |
| Raber | Radar | Rafe |
| Rabey | Radcliff | Raffaela |
| Rabun | Radcliffe | Rafferty |
| Raccaro | Radelle | Rafi |
| Race | Rade'Lle | Raford |
| Racer | Rader | Raft |
| Rachael | Radford | Raftery |
| Racheal | Radius | Rageana |
| Racheall | Radka | Ragland |
| Rachee | Radley | Ragz |
| Rachel | Radner | Raheem |
| Rachele | Radonda | Rahel |
| Rachelle | Radonovich | Rahim |
| Rachie | Radonski | Rahm |
| Racinda | Rae | Rahman |
| Racine | Raed | Rahmatollah |
| Rack | Raeford | Rahsaan |
| Rackette | Raekwon | Rail |
| Rackleff | Raelynne | Rain |
| Racquel | Raetta | Raina |
| Rad | Raevilla | Rainbow |
| Radach | Rafael | Raindrop |

| | | |
|---|---|---|
| Raineer | Ramona | Randy |
| Raines | Ramond | Ranee |
| Raini | Ramonda | Ranes |
| Rainier | Ramonde | Range |
| Rainy | Ramos | Ranger |
| Rairdan | Ramp | Rangie |
| Raisa | Ramsdell | Rangle |
| Raisin | Ramsed | Rango |
| Raj | Ramsey | Ranhall |
| Raja | Ramstad | Rani |
| Rajah | Ramstead | Rania |
| Rakel | Ramsted | Rank |
| Rakhel | Ramunda | Rankin |
| Rakowski | Ran | Ranna |
| Rakoz | Rana | Ranor |
| Raleigh | Ranata | Ransier |
| Ralkey | Rance | Ransley |
| Ralls | Ranch | Ransom |
| Rally | Rand | Ransome |
| Ralph | Randa | Ranta |
| Ralphsephine | Randal | Raokhshna |
| Ralston | Randalf | Raoul |
| Ralynn | Randall | Raphael |
| Ram | Randazzo | Rapid |
| Rama | Randel | Rapido |
| Ramanjit | Randell | Rapp |
| Rambo | Randen | Rappe |
| Ramboo | Randett | Rapture |
| Rami | Randi | Raquel |
| Ramie | Randich | Raquelle |
| Ramin | Randie | Raquiella |
| Ramiro | Randolf | Rarrick |
| Ramla | Randolph | Rasaie |
| Ramon | Random | Rasar |

| | | |
|---|---|---|
| Rascal | Rawlings | Reardan |
| Rascale | Rawlins | Reardon |
| Rash | Rawson | Reason |
| Rashad | Ray | Reaume |
| Rashawn | Rayburn | Reaza |
| Rasheda | Rayford | Reba |
| Rasheed | Rayland | Rebbie |
| Rashida | Raymon | Rebeca |
| Raskell | Raymond | Rebecah |
| Rasmus | Raymundo | Rebecca |
| Rasmussen | Rayna | Rebeka |
| Rasor | Raynaldo | Rebekah |
| Ratan | Raynard | Rebekka |
| Ratcliff | Rayne | Rebekke |
| Rate | Rayner | Rebel |
| Rathbun | Raynes | Rebeque |
| Ratheu | Raynette | Recent |
| Raton | Raynham | Record |
| Rattan | Raynor | Recorde |
| Ratton | Rayon | Red |
| Raul | Rayshawn | Redd |
| Raustin | Rayton | Reddell |
| Rave | Raz | Redden |
| Ravel | Razin | Redding |
| Raven | Razor | Reddy |
| Ravena | Rea | Redell |
| Ravenna | Reach | Redfield |
| Ravens | Read | Redford |
| Ravi | Reagan | Redgrave |
| Ravia | Real | Redken |
| Ravilla | Realize | Redman |
| Ravine | Realty | Redmon |
| Ravon | Ream | Redmond |
| Rawlin | Reames | Ree |

Reeba
Reebok
Reece
Reed
Reeder
Reeds
Reef
Reel
Reena
Rees
Reese
Reeson
Reeves
Reflect
Reflection
Reflections
Refugio
Regal
Regala
Regan
Regency
Regester
Reggie
Reghina
Regina
Reginal
Reginald
Regine
Reginia
Regis
Register
Reglin
Regon
Rehbierg

Rehbun
Rehburg
Rehnstrom
Reia
Reichel
Reichelderfer
Reichter
Reid
Reidsville
Reif
Reiko
Reiley
Reilly
Reime
Reina
Reinald
Reinaldo
Reine
Reiner
Reinette
Reingold
Reinhart
Reinhild
Reinhold
Reini
Reino
Reisen
Reister
Reith
Reitz
Releanse
Release
Reliance
Religion

Rella
Reller
Remagen
Remember
Remembrance
Remi
Remington
Remitz
Remmington
Remote
Rempfer
Remsen
Remus
Rena
Renae
Renagh
Renai
Renata
Renate
Renato
Rench
Rendell
Rendon
Rene
Renea
Renee
Reneg
Renegade
Renfro
Renhard
Renie
Renita
Rennaker
Rennebohm

Rennick

Rennie

Renny

Reno

Renshaw

Renton

Renyan

Renz

Reola

Rep

Repeat

Repet

Report

Repton

Resella

Reserve

Resi

Resort

Ressie

Rest

Reston

Reta

Reth

Retha

Retherford

Retta

Return

Reuben

Reuel

Reva

Revay

Revel

Revelation

Revell

Reven

Revere

Revilla

Revis

Revven

Reward

Rex

Rexanna

Rexford

Rey

Rey Lynn

Rey-Com

Reyes

Reyna

Reynaldo

Reynold

Reynolds

Reyshal

Reza

Rhadell

Rhea

Rheannon

Rheba

Rheland

Rhett

Rhiannon

Rhilea

Rhiley

Rhine

Rhineholdt

Rho

Rhoades

Rhoda

Rhode

Rhode Island

Rhodes

Rhodia

Rhody

Rhonda

Rhy

Rhyland

Rhynalds

Rhyne

Rhys

Rhythem

Rhythm

Ria

Ría

Rian

Riannon

Riat

Ribbon

Riblett

Ribqah

Ribreau

Ric

Rica

Ricardo

Ricarte

Rice

Rich

Richard

Richards

Richardson

Richart

Richelle

Richer

Richie

| | | |
|---|---|---|
| Richland | Rileigh | Ritchie |
| Richmond | Riley | Rite |
| Richter | Rill | Rito |
| Rick | Rilla | Ritter |
| Rickert | Rille | Ritz |
| Rickey | Rillie | Ritzman |
| Ricki | Rilling | Riv |
| Rickie | Rina | Riva |
| Rickman | Rinallo | River |
| Ricky | Rinde | Rivera |
| Rico | Rinehard | Riverina |
| Ride | Rinehart | Riverrose |
| Rider | Rinehold | Riverside |
| Ridge | Ring | Riverton |
| Ridger | Ringwald | Rivien |
| Riebold | Rinker | Riviera |
| Riedner | Rino | Rivine |
| Rieland | Rio | Rivinet |
| Riesen | Rioghach | Rivkah |
| Rifel | Riona | Rix |
| Riffle | Rios | Rixie |
| Rift | Rip | Rize |
| Rifton | Ripisal | Rjios |
| Rigel | Ripp | Road |
| Riggins | Risa | Roade |
| Riggs | Rise | Roads |
| Right | Risetti | Roald |
| Righteous | Rishan | Roalkvam |
| Rightly | Rising | Roam |
| Rigoberto | Riska | Roan |
| Rihana | Risley | Roanne |
| Riita | Riston | Roanoke |
| Riker | Rit | Roark |
| Rikki | Rita | Roatha |

Rob
Robb
Robbi
Robbia
Robbie
Robbin
Robbins
Robby
Robe
Robena
Robert
Roberta
Roberto
Roberts
Robertson
Robia
Robie
Robin
Robina
Robine
Robineettee
Robinette
Robinia
Robinson
Robles
Robson
Roby
Robyn
Roc
Rocco
Roce
Roche
Rochella
Rochelle

Rochette
Rochon
Rocio
Rock
Rockefeller
Rocket
Rockett
Rockette
Rockewell
Rockies
Rockport
Rockston
Rockwell
Rocky
Rod
Rodda
Roddick
Rode
Rodeheaver
Rodenbough
Rodeo
Rode'O
Roderick
Rodes
Rodessa
Rodger
Rodgers
Rodin
Rodlend
Rodman
Rodney
Rodolfo
Rodrick
Rodrigo

Rodriguez
Rodyo
Roe
Roediger
Roehr
Roel
Roen
Roening
Roesli
Roetter
Roff
Rogelio
Roger
Rogers
Rogette
Roggenback
Roglin
Roglins
Rogstad
Rohan
Rohmer
Rohr
Rohwer
Roine
Roisen
Roisin
Roki
Roland
Rolanda
Rolando
Roldan
Rolen
Rolette
Rolex

| | | |
|---|---|---|
| Rolf | Ronan | Rosalia |
| Rolfe | Ronda | Rosalie |
| Rolfer | Rondeau | Rosalin |
| Rolin | Rondi | Rosalind |
| Roll | Ronee | Rosalinda |
| Rolla | Ronika | Rosaline |
| Rollan | Ronit | Rosalyn |
| Rolland | Ronk | Rosamond |
| Roller | Ronna | Rosamunda |
| Rollette | Ronnie | Rosana |
| Rollie | Ronny | Rosane |
| Rollin | Roo | Rosanna |
| Rolls | Roone | Rosanne |
| Rolstad | Rooney | Rosario |
| Rolston | Roos | Rosco |
| Roma | Roose | Roscoe |
| Romaine | Roosevelt | Roscow |
| Roman | Roosma | Rose |
| Romance | Root | Roseann |
| Romanchock | Rope | Roseanne |
| Rome | Ropen | Rosebelle |
| Romeo | Ropin | Roseberry |
| Romero | Rora | Roseburg |
| Romesco | Rorie | Roseet |
| Romie | Rory | Roselie |
| Romine | Ros | Roselin |
| Romo | Rosa | Rosella |
| Romona | Rosabel | Roselle |
| Romonda | Rosabella | Roselyn |
| Romulus | Rosabelle | Rosemarie |
| Romy | Rosale | Rosemary |
| Ron | Rosalea | Rosemin |
| Rona | Rosalee | Rosen |
| Ronald | Rosaleen | Rosena |

Rosencrans
Rosendo
Rosengren
Rosetta
Rosette
Rosevear
Rosevelt
Rosi
Rosia
Rosie
Rosina
Rosine
Rosita
Roslie
Roslin
Roslyn
Roslynd
Rosman
Ross
Rossell
Rosser
Rossetti
Rossi
Rossie
Rossit
Rossiter
Rosslynne
Rosston
Rostand
Rostberg
Rostedt
Rosten
Rostor
Rostov

Roswell
Rosy
Rouge
Rough
Rouse
Roush
Rouska
Rovin
Rowan
Rowe
Rowellen
Rowen
Rowena
Rower
Rowland
Rowy
Rox
Roxana
Roxane
Roxann
Roxanna
Roxanne
Roxene
Roxette
Roxie
Roxine
Roxy
Roy
Royal
Royalty
Roybal
Royce
Roye
Roylance

Royse
Roz
Roza
Rozalie
Rozalile
Rozalin
Rozel
Rozele
Rozella
Rozina
Rozy
Rozzano
Ruari
Rube
Ruben
Rubetta
Rubia
Rubie
Rubin
Rubstello
Ruby
Rubye
Ruchert
Rucker
Rucki
Ruda
Rudan
Ruddal
Ruddell
Rudeen
Ruderman
Rudesill
Rudger
Rudker

| | | |
|---|---|---|
| Rudolf | Runner | Rutker |
| Rudolph | Ruperette | Rutland |
| Rudy | Rupert | Rutledge |
| Rue | Ruperta | Rutz |
| Rueben | Rupetta | Ruzanna |
| Rued | Rusan | Ruzen |
| Ruer | Rush | Ruzicka |
| Ruffalo | Rusher | Rwana |
| Ruffino | Rushton | Rwanda |
| Ruffle | Russ | Ryan |
| Rufus | Russel | Rycraft |
| Rugh | Russell | Rydell |
| Ruhmer | Russick | Ryder |
| Ruhoff | Russio | Rye |
| Ruhsenberger | Rust | Ryelle |
| Ruita | Rusted | Rygel |
| Ruker | Rustin | Rykeil |
| Rukeyser | Ruston | Rylaarsdam |
| Ruler | Rusty | Rylan |
| Rulon | Ruta | Rylee |
| Rumer | Rutanya | Ryley |
| Rumford | Rutch | Rylie |
| Rumina | Rutcher | Ryne |
| Rumor | Ruter | Ryser |
| Rumour | Ruth | Ryson |
| Rumston | Ruthe | Rysted |
| Runa | Rutherford | Ryta |
| Runion | Ruthia | Ryton |
| Runkel | Ruthie | |

S is for the "Soft, Sweet Smell" of your skin,
from your little round belly to your wee double chin.

| | | |
|---|---|---|
| Sa'Ud | Sachse | Safety |
| Saab | Sackat | Saffle |
| Saad | Sackett | Saffron |
| Saalfeld | Saco | Safi |
| Saba | Sada | Safia |
| Sabana | Sade | Safka |
| Sabboubeh | Sadella | Safren |
| Sabel | Sadhbh | Sagdahl |
| Sabie | Sadia | Sage |
| Sabin | Sadie | Sagely |
| Sabina | Sadik | Sager |
| Sabine | Sadika | Sahara |
| Sable | Sadler | Sahari |
| Sabong | Sadye | Sail |
| Sabra | Saeed | Saille |
| Sabraton | Saeede | Saint |
| Sabre | Saenz | Saira |
| Sabrina | Saeran | Sairto |
| Sacajawea | Saeta | Sak |
| Sacaton | Safari | Sakamoto |
| Sacco | Safe | Sakhalin |
| Sacha | Safely | Saks |

| | | |
|---|---|---|
| Sal | Sallum | Samblis |
| Salah | Sally | Samera |
| Salaidh | Salma | Sami |
| Sa'Lame | Salmon | Samih |
| Sa'Lave | Salo | Samir |
| Salazar | Salom | Samira |
| Salcha | Saloma | Sammamish |
| Salden | Salome | Sammeejo |
| Sale | Salomee | Sammie |
| Salee | Salomi | Sammy |
| Saleh | Salomone | Samo |
| Salem | Salonen | Samoa |
| Salen | Salsiburg | Samon |
| Salerno | Salsman | Samos |
| Sales | Salstrom | Samplawski |
| Salesky | Salt | Sampson |
| Salfer | Salter | Samson |
| Salhi | Saltillo | Samu |
| Salick | Salty | Samuel |
| Saliha | Salute | Samuelson |
| Salim | Salvador | San |
| Salima | Salvaggi | Sana |
| Salin | Salvation | Sanborn |
| Salina | Salvatore | Sanchez |
| Salinas | Salyer | Sand |
| Saline | Salzar | Sanda |
| Salisbury | Salzer | Sandal |
| Salish | Sam | Sandall |
| Sall | Samaha | Sandberg |
| Sallee | Samal | Sande |
| Salley | Samantha | Sandecker |
| Sallie | Samanthy | Sandell |
| Sallo | Samara | Sander |
| Salloum | Samba | Sanderfer |

Sanders
Sanderson
Sandgren
Sandi
Sandie
Sandifer
Sandle
Sandor
Sandra
Sandro
Sands
Sandstrom
Sandy
Sandy-Lee
Sanford
Sang
Sangani
Sanger
Sangre
Sanguino
Sanibel
Sanity
Sanna
Sanoy
Sanskrit
Sant
Santa
Santana
Santee
Santiago
Santina
Santo
Santos
Sanura

Sapinoso
Sapphire
Sappho
Sara
Sarafein
Sarafine
Sarah
Sarai
Saran
Saranac
Sarasota
Sarat
Saratoga
Sardinia
Sardis
Sarene
Sarette
Sargent
Sarhan
Sari
Sarina
Sarine
Sarita
Sarles
Sarnia
Saron
Sarpy
Sarrah
Sarten
Sarth
Sarton
Sartwell
Sarvinski
Sasa

Sasha
Sashida
Saskatoon
Sassoon
Satak
Satalick
Sater
Sathers
Satilite
Satin
Sation
Satsop
Sattler
Satu
Saturday
Saturn
Saturnalia
Satyr
Sauce
Saud
Saude
Saudi
Sauer
Sauk
Saul
Saulk
Sauna
Saunders
Saundra
Sauri
Saurio
Sauriol
Sauron
Sausele

| | | |
|---|---|---|
| Sausolito | Scandal | Schiller |
| Savage | Scandia | Schillereff |
| Savana | Scania | Schilling |
| Savanah | Scanlon | Schillinger |
| Savanna | Scapula | Schindler |
| Savannah | Scarborough | Schlatter |
| Savary | Scarlett | Schlechten |
| Save | Scene | Schleichert |
| Savena | Scenery | Schlender |
| Saver | Scenic | Schloe |
| Savery | Sceta | Schlonga |
| Saville | Schaan | Schloss |
| Savina | Schade | Schmertz |
| Savona | Schadrach | Schmidt |
| Savone | Schaefer | Schmitt |
| Savory | Schafer | Schmitz |
| Sawatch | Schaffer | Schmoker |
| Sawer | Schafi | Schneider |
| Sawich | Schaftlein | Schoesler |
| Sawyer | Schartung | Schoessler |
| Sax | Schauer | Schofield |
| Saxe | Schave | Scholl |
| Saxis | Scheel | Scholten |
| Sayer | Schei | School |
| Sayler | Scheil | Schoonover |
| Sayles | Scheild | Schrader |
| Sayre | Schenk | Schraeder |
| Sblendorio | Scheuermann | Schraw |
| Scafturon | Scheuffele | Schriver |
| Scale | Schiavo | Schroder |
| Scaler | Schicchi | Schroedel |
| Scamp | Schick | Schroeder |
| Scamper | Schield | Schuerhoff |
| Scan | Schierberg | Schufreider |

| | | |
|---|---|---|
| Schug | Scuba | Sebika |
| Schulke | Scubby | Sebuka |
| Schuller | Scully | Secant |
| Schultz | Sea | Secena |
| Schulyer | Seabisquit | Second |
| Schumacher | Seabrook | Secont |
| Schurman | Seaforth | Secrest |
| Schutt | Seager | Secret |
| Schutter | Seagull | Secrist |
| Schutz | Seal | Secunda |
| Schuyler | Sealor | Secure |
| Schwantes | Seals | Security |
| Schwartz | Sealy | Seda |
| Sciamanda | Seamus | Sedan |
| Science | Sean | Sedanca |
| Scirleah | Search | Sedancia |
| Sclera | Searia | Seday |
| Scoby | Searlait | Sedge |
| Scoll | Searles | Sedgewick |
| Scoot | Sears | Sedley |
| Scooter | Seaside | Sedona |
| Scope | Season | Sedrata |
| Scorpio | Season's | Sedrick |
| Scot | Seatco | Sedro |
| Scotch | Seater | Sedy |
| Scotland | Seaton | Seed |
| Scott | Seattle | Seedy |
| Scottie | Seaver | Seek |
| Scotty | Seb | Seeker |
| Scout | Sebade | Seelette |
| Scranton | Sebago | Seeley |
| Scratch | Sebaska | Seelie |
| Screen | Sebastian | Seely |
| Scub | Sebastopol | Seff |

| | | |
|---|---|---|
| Segal | Selin | Senn |
| Segami | Selina | Sennet |
| Seguin | Selinda | Seno |
| Segunda | Selio | Senovia |
| Sehlin | Selk | Senria |
| Seiber | Selkirk | Sense |
| Seibor | Sell | Sensen |
| Seiger | Sellar | Sensimila |
| Seigle | Sellers | Sensimillia |
| Seiko | Sellman | Senson |
| Seil | Sellor | Sensory |
| Seilah | Selma | Sentar |
| Seiler | Selmer | Sentara |
| Seilor | Selove | Sentari |
| Seine | Selstead | Sentaur |
| Seismic | Selton | Sentence |
| Seitz | Selvarajo | Sentenn |
| Seize | Selz | Sentry |
| Sela | Semaj | Senville |
| Selby | Semanko | Senyitko |
| Selden | Semi | Sephana |
| Seldo | Sen | Sephen |
| Seldom | Sena | Sepia |
| Seldovia | Senalde | September |
| Sele | Senario | Septima |
| Select | Senaro | Septo |
| Selena | Senator | Sequeira |
| Selene | Send | Sequim |
| Selera | Sendal | Sequin |
| Seleria | Senden | Sequoia |
| Self | Sender | Ser |
| Selia | Seneca | Serafin |
| Selie | Senegal | Serafinase |
| Selimah | Senegali | Seraphina |

| | | |
|---|---|---|
| Serena | Several | Shakto |
| Serene | Severn | Shaktolik |
| Serenity | Severson | Shala |
| Sergeant | Severtson | Shalane |
| Sergei | Sevier | Shale |
| Sergel | Sevit | Shalear |
| Serger | Sevitt | Shaley |
| Sergio | Sexton | Shalom |
| Serious | Seyl | Shalonda |
| Serita | Seyler | Shamar |
| Sermon | Seyller | Shameka |
| Sermonti | Seymour | Shamika |
| Sern | Shabella | Shamina |
| Serpens | Shaboom | Shamp |
| Serpent | Shabro | Shamps |
| Serpico | Shack | Shamu |
| Serra | Shackelton | Shamus |
| Serria | Shad | Shana |
| Serry | Shade | Shance |
| Service | Shadoff | Shanda |
| Sesame | Shadon | Shandera |
| Sesha | Shadow | Shandy |
| Seshona | Shady | Shane |
| Sesi | Shaffer | Shani |
| Setcka | Shai | Shania |
| Seth | Shain | Shanice |
| Setka | Shaina | Shanika |
| Setler | Shaine | Shaniko |
| Sett | Shak | Shaniqua |
| Setter | Shaken | Shanita |
| Settig | Shakera | Shanna |
| Settle | Shakespeare | Shannah |
| Seul | Shakira | Shannan |
| Seven | Shaklawun | Shannon |

| | | |
|---|---|---|
| Shanon | Sharyl | Sheaffer |
| Shanta | Shasanna | Sheahan |
| Shante | Shasta | Shear |
| Shantel | Shatner | Sheat |
| Shantell | Shatto | Sheba |
| Shantelle | Shattuck | Shed |
| Shanty | Shaun | Sheedy |
| Shapansky | Shauna | Sheela |
| Shaper | Shaunavon | Sheelagh |
| Shaquille | Shaundra | Sheelah |
| Shar | Shauntee | Sheena |
| Shara | Shave | Sheenagh |
| Sharan | Shavers | Sheer |
| Sharar | Shaw | Sheeton |
| Shari | Shawanda | Sheets |
| Sharif | Shawley | Sheffield |
| Shariff | Shawn | Sheik |
| Sharise | Shawna | Sheila |
| Sharisteem | Shawnacee | Shel |
| Shark | Shawnen | Shela |
| Sharkey | Shawver | Shelagh |
| Sharla | Shay | Shelbi |
| Sharleen | Shayde | Shelbie |
| Sharlene | Shayden | Shelburne |
| Sharlet | Shaye | Shelby |
| Sharline | Shayla | Sheldon |
| Sharon | Shayli | Shelf |
| Sharona | Shaylise | Shelia |
| Sharonda | Shayna | Shelina |
| Sharp | Shayne | Shell |
| Sharrah | Shazam | Shella |
| Sharrlyn | She | Shellee |
| Sharron | Shea | Shellenberger |
| Sharti | Sheaf | Shelley |

| | | |
|---|---|---|
| Shelli | Sherrie | Ship |
| Shellie | Sherrif | Shipe |
| Shelly | Sherrill | Shipley |
| Shelt | Sherry | Shire |
| Shelter | Sherwood | Shireen |
| Shelton | Sherye | Shirin |
| Shena | Sheryl | Shirk |
| Shenandoah | Sheryll | Shirl |
| Shendi | Shevis | Shirlee |
| Shep | Shevlin | Shirlene |
| Shepard | Shevon | Shirley |
| Shepherd | Shevron | Shirlie |
| Shephers | Sheyenne | Shirra |
| Shepley | Shiela | Shirrilla |
| Sheppard | Shield | Shiseido |
| Sher | Shields | Shisler |
| Sheraton | Shiferaw | Shiva |
| Sherborn | Shila | Shivananda |
| Sheree | Shilah | Shiver |
| Sherene | Shilbayeh | Shkhara |
| Sheri | Shillan | Shnoe |
| Sheridan | Shilman | Sho |
| Sherie | Shilo | Shoal |
| Sherif | Shiloh | Shoales |
| Sheriff | Shim | Sholes |
| Sheril | Shimmer | Shoma |
| Sherilyn | Shimmy | Shomshor |
| Sherion | Shimon | Shon |
| Sherita | Shin | Shonda |
| Sherkat | Shina | Shonna |
| Sherlock | Shine | Shontae |
| Sherm | Shining | Shontal |
| Sherman | Shinsing | Shontina |
| Sherri | Shiny | Shoop |

Shop
Shope
Shore
Short
Shorty
Shoshana
Shoshannah
Shotton
Shoun
Shover
Show
Shrader
Shreve
Shrout
Shu-Chin
Shue
Shuler
Shull
Shults
Shultz
Shumaker
Shuman
Shumate
Shuming
Shumway
Shupert
Shurtliff
Shushannah
Shustak
Shute
Shutter
Shyanne
Shye
Shyler

Shylock
Sial
Siam
Sian
Siano
Sias
Siatco
Sibbett
Sibeal
Sibelle
Siberia
Sibil
Sibille
Sibold
Sibyl
Sibyll
Sibylla
Sibylle
Sicily
Sicor
Sid
Siddiqui
Siddon
Side
Sides
Sidney
Sidor
Siegel
Siegmeth
Sieland
Sielbach
Sieler
Siena
Sienkiewich

Sienko
Sienna
Siero
Sierra
Sierto
Siesling
Siever
Sievers
Sifer
Sifton
Sig
Sigel
Sigfried
Sigge
Sighile
Siglal
Siglane
Sigmon
Sigmund
Sign
Signa
Signal
Signale
Signature
Signe
Signey
Sigourney
Sigrid
Sigurd
Sikes
Sikeston
Siki
Siko
Sikos

Sil
Silas
Silcon
Sile
Sileas
Silence
Silent
Silesia
Siletz
Silevra
Silhouette
Silica
Silins
Silk
Silky
Sills
Silo
Siloyant
Silva
Silvan
Silvana
Silve
Silver
Silveria
Silverman
Silves
Silvia
Silvie
Silvio
Silvonen
Silvria
Sim
Simaron
Simba

Simcoe
Simek
Simeon
Simera
Simescu
Simienta
Similar
Simile
Simmer
Simmonds
Simmons
Simms
Simon
Simona
Simone
Simonea
Simonette
Simoni
Simonia
Simonne
Simons
Simonsen
Simonson
Simple
Simplicity
Simpson
Sims
Sinbad
Sincere
Sincerity
Sinclair
Sinden
Sindle
Sindy

Sine
Sinead
Sing
Singer
Singh
Sining
Sinn
Sinnott
Sintha
Sinu
Sio
Siobhan
Sion
Sioux
Sipe
Sipher
Sipp
Sir
Sire
Siren
Siri
Sirn
Sirna
Sirotnikova
Sis
Sisco
Sise
Sisemac
Sisemia
Sisi
Sisie
Sisile
Sisku
Sissey

Sisson
Sissy
Sister
Sisterly
Sistine
Sitca
Sitch
Site
Sith
Sitka
Sitton
Siubhan
Siuki
Siusaidh
Siusan
Siv
Siva
Sivaneswaran
Sivertson
Sivney
Siwah
Six
Sizer
Sizmic
Sjolander
Skaggs
Skalicky
Skate
Skeels
Skeet
Skemp
Skewis
Ski
Skilar

Skiles
Skiller
Skinner
Skip
Skirko
Skoglund
Skopie
Sky
Skye
Skyla
Skylar
Skyler
Slade
Slakey
Slam
Slana
Slat
Slate
Slater
Slaton
Slavicek
Slawin
Slaybaugh
Slayr
Sledge
Sleep
Sleet
Slemmer
Sletten
Slevon
Slevough
Slid
Slide
Slidell

Sliker
Slim
Sliva
Sliver
Sloan
Sloane
Slocan
Slogan
Slope
Slow
Slueima
Slug
Slusser
Slym
Small
Smalley
Smelser
Smeltzer
Smet
Smick
Smile
Smiler
Smiley
Smith
Smitti
Smitty
Smoke
Smoky
Smudge
Smythe
Snail
Snake
Snaza
Snee

| | | |
|---|---|---|
| Snelson | Sokolowski | Sonja |
| Snicker | Sol | Sonnet |
| Snider | Solace | Sonny |
| Sniezak | Solar | Sonoma |
| Sniglet | Solaria | Sonora |
| Snoma | Sole | Sontag |
| Snoqualmie | Soledad | Sonya |
| Snore | Soleil | Soo |
| Snorri | Solid | Soon |
| Snow | Solince | Sooner |
| Snowden | Solo | Soong |
| Snowe | Solomon | Sooz |
| Snowy | Solon | Soozie |
| Snych | Solstice | Soper |
| Snyder | Soma | Sopheia |
| Soap | Somali | Sophia |
| Soapy | Sombar | Sophie |
| Soar | Somber | Soprano |
| Sobol | Sombrero | Soran |
| Sobotka | Some | Sorcha |
| Sobottka | Somer | Sorel |
| Social | Somerie | Sorely |
| Soconto | Somero | Soren |
| Socorro | Somers | Sorensen |
| Socorrow | Somerset | Sorie |
| Soderlind | Someswar | Soroka |
| Soderquist | Sommer | Sorran |
| Soderstrom | Sommers | Sorrel |
| Soehl | Sommerville | Sorrow |
| Sofeia | Sondo | Sorry |
| Sofia | Sondra | Sorush |
| Sofie | Sonette | Sosanna |
| Sofy | Song | Soshana |
| Soike | Sonia | Soshannah |

Soth
Soto
Sou
Sougourany
Sougourney
Soul
Sould
Soule
Soully
Sound
Sounder
Soupy
Source
Souron
Sousley
South
South Carolina
South Dakota
Souvannakasy
Souxsie
Souza
Sovereign
Sowady
Sowards
Sowers
Spa
Space
Spacek
Spahr
Spaid
Spain
Spair
Spanel
Spangle

Spangler
Spaque
Spare
Sparea
Spargo
Sparkle
Sparks
Sparky
Sparrow
Sparta
Spartan
Spaulding
Spear
Spec
Specht
Special
Speck
Spee
Speed
Speedy
Speelman
Speer
Spellman
Spence
Spencer
Spend
Spengler
Spenser
Spensor
Spere
Sperline
Sperling
Sperlini
Spezia

Spheeris
Spica
Spice
Spicer
Spielberg
Spieler
Spigler
Spilsbury
Spilseth
Spinelli
Spipa
Spiral
Spirit
Spiro
Spitz
Spitznagel
Spivac
Split
Spokane
Spoon
Spooner
Sporseen
Sport
Sportsman
Spradin
Spradlin
Sprae
Sprague
Sprat
Spray
Sprig
Spring
Springer
Springfield

Sprinkle
Sprint
Sprite
Spritzer
Spruce
Sprya
Spurrell
Spyral
Spyrea
Squire
Sral
Srebro
Sredni
Srilanka
Sring
Stacey
Staci
Stacia
Stacie
Stacy
Staeger
Stafford
Stag
Stage
Stager
Stagger
Stahlecker
Stain
Stainá
Stainly
Staley
Stallard
Stallín
Stallings

Stallins
Stallo
Stalvic
Stamen
Stamford
Stamon
Stamp
Stamper
Stan
Stancil
Stand
Standahl
Standard
Standerford
Standford
Standifer
Standing
Standish
Stane
Stanfield
Stanford
Stang
Stange
Stanger
Stankus
Stanley
Stanleye
Stanly
Stantey
Stanton
Stanza
Staphanie
Stapleton
Stappenbeck

Star
Starick
Staricka
Starin
Stark
Starke
Starkey
Starla
Starling
Starmon
Starr
Starrla
Starry
Starshine
Starskey
Start
Stasia
State
Staten
Station
Staton
Stator
Statue
Status
Stauffer
Staunch
Staunton
Stauton
Stautumon
Stay
Staylon
Ste
Steadman
Steal

| | | |
|---|---|---|
| Stealth | Stein | Stephon |
| Stealthy | Steinbeck | Stephy |
| Steam | Steinberg | Stereo |
| Steamer | Steiner | Sterline |
| Stearns | Steinert | Sterling |
| Stebly | Steingrebe | Stern |
| Stecco | Steinman | Sterner |
| Stecher | Steinmetz | Stet |
| Steege | Steiven | Stetsen |
| Steel | Steka | Stetson |
| Steele | Steklenburg | Stettler |
| Steelie | Stell | Stevan |
| Steelton | Stella | Stevana |
| Steely | Stello | Steve |
| Steen | Stelter | Steven |
| Steep | Stem | Stevena |
| Steeple | Sten | Stevens |
| Steer | Stenback | Steveson |
| Steev | Stencil | Stevia |
| Steeve | Stensland | Stevie |
| Stef | Steph | Stevon |
| Stefan | Stepha | Stevvi |
| Stefani | Stephan | Stevvy |
| Stefania | Stephane | Stew |
| Stefanie | Stephani | Steward |
| Stefano | Stephania | Stewart |
| Stefanos | Stephanie | Stia |
| Stefany | Stephanine | Stick |
| Steffan | Stephany | Sticker |
| Steffen | Stephen | Stidham |
| Stegar | Stephenie | Stidman |
| Steiger | Stephens | Stiffel |
| Steigman | Stephie | Stiffen |
| Steigner | Stephine | Stig |

| | | |
|---|---|---|
| Stiger | Stoken | Stover |
| Stigler | Stoker | Stow |
| Stihl | Stokes | Stowe |
| Stile | Stolar | Strabb |
| Stiler | Stole | Strabbing |
| Stiles | Stolen | Strada |
| Still | Stoll | Strader |
| Stillman | Stollen | Strado |
| Stillwell | Stone | Strafford |
| Stilson | Stoneburg | Straight |
| Stilt | Stonecipher | Strait |
| Stilts | Stonewall | Straits |
| Stimberis | Stoney | Straka |
| Stimpson | Stony | Stram |
| Stimson | Stooge | Strand |
| Stina | Stopsen | Strander |
| Stine | Stopson | Stranton |
| Sting | Storage | Strasbourger |
| Stinger | Storeide | Strasburg |
| Stinson | Storey | Strasser |
| Stinton | Storkan | Strassman |
| Stiny | Storkel | Strata |
| Stipe | Storlie | Strate |
| Stirling | Storm | Strategy |
| Stiwald | Storme | Stratford |
| Stoc | Stormi | Strating |
| Stock | Stormy | Strato |
| Stockard | Story | Stratos |
| Stocker | Stott | Stratton |
| Stockman | Stotz | Stratus |
| Stockton | Stoudt | Straub |
| Stoe | Stouffer | Strauch |
| Stoffer | Stoughton | Straughn |
| Stoke | Stout | Straught |

173

| | | |
|---|---|---|
| Strauser | Stron | Stutsman |
| Strauss | Strong | Styers |
| Strawder | Stroschein | Styg |
| Strawn | Stroug | Style |
| Stray | Strozak | Styler |
| Strea | Strozyk | Styles |
| Streak | Struck | Stylette |
| Stream | Struckam | Styrone |
| Streat | Strucker | Suadano |
| Streaton | Struckman | Suade |
| Streator | Strugar | Suafoa |
| Streem | Strum | Suakin |
| Streep | Strumski | Suarez |
| Street | Strut | Sucati |
| Strehlow | Struthers | Success |
| Streib | Stryker | Such |
| Streicher | Stuart | Suchan |
| Streifel | Stuber | Sucher |
| Stretch | Stucco | Suchley |
| Strevy | Studen | Sudan |
| Strick | Studer | Sudden |
| Stricken | Studio | Sudie |
| Stricker | Study | Sue |
| Stricklan | Stueve | Suede |
| Strickland | Stuhr | Suezie |
| Strickler | Stull | Suezy |
| Strid | Stullick | Sugar |
| Strieck | Stumble | Sugarplum |
| Striet | Stump | Suing |
| Stripe | Sturdevant | Suit |
| Stritmatter | Sturgeon | Suite |
| Strobe | Sturgis | Suitor |
| Stroke | Sturn | Sujka |
| Strom | Stutch | Suke |

| | | |
|---|---|---|
| Sukey | Sundance | Susan |
| Suki | Sunday | Susana |
| Sukie | Sundberg | Susanna |
| Sula | Sunde | Susanne |
| Suleika | Sundell | Suschen |
| Sulky | Sunder | Suse |
| Sullivan | Sundial | Susetta |
| Sulllivan | Sundown | Susie |
| Sultan | Sundry | Susitna |
| Sultana | Sunface | Susman |
| Sultzer | Sunfish | Suspect |
| Sulu | Sung | Sussex |
| Sulzer | Suni | Sustain |
| Sumara | Sunny | Suszanna |
| Sumatra | Sunrae | Suszanne |
| Sumi | Sunray | Suter |
| Sumion | Sunrise | Sutera |
| Sumitomo | Sunset | Sutherland |
| Sumitow | Sunshine | Sutley |
| Summary | Sunstrom | Sutmiller |
| Summer | Suntana | Sutten |
| Summers | Suntrana | Sutter |
| Summette | Sunup | Sutteri |
| Summit | Suny | Sutton |
| Summy | Suokas | Suxannah |
| Sumner | Supensky | Suzan |
| Sump | Surely | Suzanna |
| Sumpter | Surf | Suzanne |
| Sumter | Surface | Suzelle |
| Sumutra | Surinam | Suzetta |
| Sun | Surround | Suzette |
| Sund | Survey | Suzi |
| Sundae | Surya | Suzie |
| Sundale | Susak | Suzon |

175

| | | |
|---|---|---|
| Suzuki | Sweetums | Syfer |
| Suzy | Sweety | Syle |
| Svatonsky | Sweigard | Sylena |
| Sven | Swendt | Sylesia |
| Svensen | Swenson | Sylva |
| Svenson | Swentkofske | Sylvan |
| Svoboda | Swept | Sylvana |
| Swafford | Swett | Sylvester |
| Swahili | Swidecki | Sylvia |
| Swalling | Swift | Sylvie |
| Swallow | Swifton | Sylvy |
| Swan | Swiggs | Sylwia |
| Swansea | Swim | Symbol |
| Swansen | Swingle | Symes |
| Swanson | Swires | Symone |
| Swanton | Switzer | Synchroid |
| Swart | Switzerland | Synonym |
| Swartz | Sybil | Sypher |
| Swasey | Sybilia | Syra |
| Swecker | Sybilla | Syracrus |
| Sweden | Sybille | Syrena |
| Swedon | Syble | Syria |
| Sween | Sybyl | System |
| Sweeney | Sycks | Syvania |
| Sweet | Sydnee | Syverson |
| Sweetheart | Sydney | Syx |
| Sweetie | Sydnie | Szeg |
| Sweeton | Syed | Szewcik |

T is for "Toddler," as you grow through the years.
It's off to school and someday careers.

| | | |
|---|---|---|
| Ta Ná | Taft | Talent |
| Tab | Tag | Tales |
| Tabard | Tagant | Tali |
| Tabatha | Tagent | Talia |
| Tabbi | Tagman | Taliene |
| Tabbie | Tague | Taliesin |
| Tabby | Tahance | Talisa |
| Tabi | Tahanee | Talise |
| Tabia | Tahati | Talla |
| Tabina | Tahiti | Tallahassee |
| Tabitha | Tahoe | Tallassee |
| Tabor | Tai | Talley |
| Tachell | Taiga | Talli |
| Taci | Taja | Tallib |
| Tackett | Take | Tallie |
| Tackle | Takla | Tallis |
| Tactic | Taklia | Tallman |
| Tad | Tal | Tallota |
| Tael | Talaga | Tallou |
| Taf | Talcott | Tallula |
| Taff | Tale | Tallulah |
| Tafoya | Talea | Tally |

| | | |
|---|---|---|
| Talmadge | Tampa | Taniesha |
| Talmai | Tamper | Tanijo |
| Talon | Tamra | Tanika |
| Talor | Tams | Tanis |
| Talotta | Tamsen | Tanisa |
| Talukdar | Tan | Tanish |
| Talvo | Tana | Tanisha |
| Talxott | Tanada | Tanishea |
| Talya | Tanaga | Tanishia |
| Tam | Tanager | Tanja |
| Tama | Tanagray | Tank |
| Tamaiko | Tanak | Tanna |
| Tamala | Tanaka | Tanneberg |
| Taman | Tanana | Tanner |
| Tamantha | Tanata | Tannor |
| Tamaqua | Tandi | Tansey |
| Tamaque | Tandra | Tansie |
| Tamar | Tandy | Tansy |
| Tamara | Tane | Tantum |
| Tamarind | Taneal | Tanya |
| Tamaroa | Taneisha | Tanzie |
| Tamatha | Tanesha | Tao |
| Tamber | Taneshea | Taos |
| Tambi | Taney | Tap |
| Tameka | Tanga | Tape |
| Tamela | Tangela | Tapestry |
| Tamera | Tangent | Tapia |
| Tami | Tangerine | Taplett |
| Tamie | Tangle | Tappen |
| Tamika | Tangles | Tapper |
| Tamiko | Tani | Tar |
| Tammi | Tania | Tara |
| Tammie | Tanicha | Tarah |
| Tammy | Taniesche | Tarbet |

| | | |
|---|---|---|
| Tareq | Tate | Tax |
| Targ | Tateanna | Tay |
| Targa | Tateeahna | Tayeh |
| Target | Tatem | Tayler |
| Tarheal | Tatern | Taylor |
| Tari | Tatfeld | Tayton |
| Taria | Tatiana | Taz |
| Tarim | Tatman | Tazio |
| Tariq | Tatna | Tazmin |
| Tarl | Tatum | Tazor |
| Tarmac | Tatyana | Te Né |
| Tarn | Taun | Teague |
| Taro | Taunia | Teah |
| Taronto | Taunton | Teal |
| Tarpon | Taura | Teanec |
| Tarragon | Taurean | Teanick |
| Tarrance | Taurus | Teara |
| Tarricon | Tausha | Teasdale |
| Tarry | Tauten | Teasha |
| Tarsha | Tauton | Techay |
| Tarsus | Tavares | Ted |
| Taryn | Tavi | Teddi |
| Tascer | Tavish | Teddie |
| Tascha | Tavon | Teddy |
| Tasco | Tavor | Tedra |
| Tascosa | Tavy | Teena |
| Tash | Tawana | Teenie |
| Tasha | Tawanda | Teep |
| Tashanna | Tawanna | Teeter |
| Task | Tawney | Tegeler |
| Tasker | Tawnga | Tehran |
| Tat | Tawni | Teia |
| Tatamy | Tawny | Teina |
| Tatania | Tawnya | Tejay |

| | | |
|---|---|---|
| Tekla | Tenoski | Terre |
| Telecky | Tensfeld | Terrece |
| Teleph | Tent | Terrell |
| Teleview | Teo | Terrence |
| Telissa | Teodora | Terri |
| Tellesbo | Teodoro | Terrie |
| Tellson | Teodory | Terrill |
| Telly | Tephania | Terrin |
| Telo | Tephel | Terry |
| Telpet | Tepid | Terryon |
| Telsa | Tera | Terwilliger |
| Temant | Terah | Teryall |
| Temina | Tercel | Teryann |
| Tempe | Terence | Tesch |
| Tempo | Teresa | Tesdal |
| Tempus | Terese | Tesdall |
| Tena | Teressa | Tesia |
| Tendra | Teri | Tesimony |
| Tenea | Terie | Teske |
| Tene'a | Terina | Tess |
| Tenecia | Terisa | Tessa |
| Teng | Tern | Tesseract |
| Tenille | Ternan | Tessi |
| Tenino | Terne | Tessie |
| Tenisha | Terr | Tessy |
| Tenner | Terra | Tester |
| Tennessa | Terrace | Tetlin |
| Tennessee | Terragon | Teton |
| Tennie | Terraine | Tetra |
| Tennille | Terralore | Tetz |
| Tennis | Terralynn | Tev |
| Tennor | Terran | Teva |
| Tenon | Terrance | Teven |
| Tenor | Terrane | Tevia |

| | | |
|---|---|---|
| Tevin | Their | Thomasina |
| Tevis | Theison | Thompsen |
| Tex | Thekla | Thompson |
| Texas | Thele | Thomsen |
| Texon | Thelma | Thomson |
| Teyah | Thelson | Thona |
| Thackeray | Thena | Thonda |
| Thad | Theo | Thor |
| Thaddeus | Theodora | Thora |
| Thai | Theodore | Thorald |
| Thalia | Theodosia | Thorn |
| Thalman | Theola | Thornburg |
| Thamer | Theophrania | Thorndike |
| Thames | Theory | Thorne |
| Than | There | Thorniley |
| Thane | Theresa | Thornson |
| Thanh | Therese | Thornton |
| Thank | Theresia | Thorp |
| Thanks | Theron | Thorpe |
| Thao | Therson | Thorson |
| Tharmalinga | They | Thorton |
| Tharo | Thibaudeau | Thought |
| Tharp | Thiel | Thousand |
| Tharpe | Thiele | Thrace |
| Thatch | Thielen | Thrall |
| Thatcher | Thielsen | Thread |
| Thaydra | Thiessen | Three |
| Thayer | Thill | Threlkeld |
| Thayne | Thing | Thresa |
| Thazon | This | Thrill |
| Thea | Thistle | Throckmorton |
| Theadore | Tho | Throne |
| Theda | Thom | Throw |
| Theia | Thomas | Thrseus |

| | | |
|---|---|---|
| Thrush | Tie | Tilo |
| Thunder | Tiedemann | Tilse |
| Thurlon | Tieman | Tilsit |
| Thurman | Tiennette | Tilson |
| Thurmond | Tienniette | Tilston |
| Thursa | Tiera | Tilt |
| Thursday | Tierney | Tim |
| Thursielou | Tierra | Timb |
| Thurston | Tierre | Timber |
| Thuton | Tietge | Time |
| Thy | Tieton | Timely |
| Thyme | Tifany | Timer |
| Thyra | Tiff | Timex |
| Tia | Tiffani | Timi |
| Tiago | Tiffanie | Timina |
| Tiajuana | Tiffany | Timm |
| Tiana | Tiffie | Timmelyn |
| Tianna | Tiffin | Timmie |
| Tiara | Tiffy | Timmon |
| Tibbie | Tifton | Timmons |
| Tibbs | Tigara | Timmothy |
| Tibet | Tigard | Timmy |
| Tice | Tiger | Timon |
| Ticey | Tighe | Timothea |
| Ticha | Tihai | Timothy |
| Ticia | Tihati | Tina |
| Tickle | Tike | Tincher |
| Tickles | Tiki | Tindall |
| Tidal | Tikka | Tinelle |
| Tide | Tilahun | Tingley |
| Tidelands | Tiller | Tinka |
| Tider | Tilley | Tinte |
| Tides | Tillie | Tinx |
| Tidy | Tillman | Tiny |

| | | |
|---|---|---|
| Tioga | Tobey | Tomato |
| Tiozah | Tobias | Tomeka |
| Tip | Tobin | Tomi |
| Tipler | Toby | Tomika |
| Tipon | Tod | Tommie |
| Tiptoe | Today | Tommy |
| Tipton | Todd | Tomorra |
| Tirane | Tode | Tomorrow |
| Tire | Todo | Toms |
| Tiree | Todorovich | Tone |
| Tirest | Tody | Toney |
| Tiro | Toe | Tonga |
| Tirsa | Tognocchi | Toni |
| Tisa | Togo | Tonia |
| Tisdale | Tohedd | Tonie |
| Tish | Toiresa | Tonja |
| Tisha | Tokala | Tony |
| Tishia | Tokio | Tonya |
| Tita | Tolar | Tonyalee |
| Titan | Toledo | Tonye |
| Titania | Toleta | Tooger |
| Titanium | Toletta | Toohey |
| Tithia | Tolette | Took |
| Title | Toll | Top |
| Tito | Tolland | Topaz |
| Tittemore | Tolliver | Toque |
| Titterness | Tolly | Tor |
| Titus | Tolmie | Tora |
| To | Tolon | Toralf |
| Toad | Tom | Torch |
| Toast | Tomara | Tore |
| Tobacco | Tomas | Torell |
| Tobe | Tomasa | Toreno |
| Toberer | Tomaso | Torey |

| | | |
|---|---|---|
| Torgerson | Towell | Traffic |
| Torgeson | Tower | Trafton |
| Tori | Towhead | Traia |
| Torino | Town | Trail |
| Torkko | Towner | Trailer |
| Torn | Townes | Trails |
| Torna | Townley | Trainer |
| Tornado | Towns | Trali |
| Tornato | Townsend | Tran |
| Toro | Toy | Transit |
| Toronto | Toya | Trap |
| Torra | Toyon | Trapper |
| Torrance | Toyra | Tras |
| Torrant | Trabant | Trask |
| Torrent | Trabi | Trautman |
| Torrero | Tracá | Trave |
| Torres | Trace | Travel |
| Torrey | Traceá | Traveler |
| Torrez | Tracee | Traver |
| Torrin | Traceton | Travers |
| Torry | Tracey | Traverse |
| Tory | Traci | Travese |
| Tosha | Tracie | Travess |
| Tostig | Tracion | Travi |
| Toston | Track | Travis |
| Touche | Tract | Travon |
| Tour | Traction | Trawle |
| Touraine | Tracton | Tray |
| Tova | Tracy | Traylor |
| Tove | Trade | Traynham |
| Tow | Tradition | Traynor |
| Towana | Tradz | Trayson |
| Towe | Trae | Trayton |
| Towel | Traer | Tre |

| | | |
|---|---|---|
| Trea | Trevon | Trip |
| Treasure | Trevor | Tripo |
| Treasureann | Trey | Tripper |
| Tree | Treyson | Trish |
| Treese | Treyten | Trisha |
| Treichel | Treytin | Trishia |
| Treinen | Treyton | Triss |
| Treiner | Tri | Trissi |
| Trek | Trial | Trissie |
| Tremaine | Trian | Trissy |
| Tremayne | Triana | Trista |
| Tremblay | Tribune | Tristan |
| Tremont | Tricia | Triste |
| Tremonton | Trick | Tristen |
| Trena | Tricola | Tristian |
| Trench | Tricor | Tristin |
| Trend | Trident | Triston |
| Trenda | Triest'E | Triton |
| Trent | Triex | Triumph |
| Trenter | Trift | Trix |
| Trenton | Trifton | Trixie |
| Trepanier | Trillion | Trixy |
| Trerice | Trillium | Trodahl |
| Tres | Trimmer | Trojan |
| Tresa | Trina | Trolley |
| Tresedder | Trinadade | Trommer |
| Tressa | Trine | Trona |
| Tressie | Trinette | Tronsit |
| Trestle | Trinh | Tronson |
| Treva | Trini | Troop |
| Trever | Trinidad | Trooper |
| Trevin | Trinity | Trop |
| Trevino | Trinka | Tropeano |
| Trevis | Trio | Trosper |

| | | |
|---|---|---|
| Trot | Tubalcain | Tupling |
| Trotter | Tubes | Tuppence |
| Trouble | Tuc | Turck |
| Troupe | Tucker | Turgid |
| Trout | Tucson | Turin |
| Trowbridge | Tud | Turk |
| Trowel | Tudi | Turkey |
| Troy | Tudley | Turlocke |
| Truck | Tuella | Turn |
| Trucker | Tuesday | Turnbull |
| Truda | Tulare | Turner |
| Trude | Tule | Turnley |
| Trudel | Tuledo | Turon |
| Trudi | Tulissa | Turone |
| Trudie | Tull | Turquoise |
| Trudy | Tullar | Turrell |
| True | Tullee | Tuscarora |
| Truemary | Tulley | Tushing |
| Truman | Tullis | Tuson |
| Trumble | Tully | Tustin |
| Trunk | Tulsa | Tut |
| Truong | Tulsanne | Tuttle |
| Truro | Tululah | Tux |
| Trussler | Tululaha | Tuxedo |
| Trust | Tululu | Tveten |
| Truth | Tumble | Twananha |
| Try | Tundra | Twanoh |
| Trygvee | Tune | Twanoha |
| Tryon | Tuney | Tweed |
| Trysta | Tungston | Tweit |
| Trystin | Tuni | Twig |
| Tsarina | Tunis | Twigg |
| Tschirgi | Tunisia | Twiggy |
| Tuan | Tunnel | Twila |

| | | |
|---|---|---|
| Twilaine | Tyesha | Tyone |
| Twilic | Tyfany | Type |
| Twilight | Tyffany | Typee |
| Twin | Tygart | Typha |
| Twitch | Tygh | Typhoon |
| Twitcher | Tyke | Tyquan |
| Two | Tylar | Tyr |
| Twyla | Tyler | Tyra |
| Twyle | Tylor | Tyree |
| Twylla | Tyme | Tyreece |
| Twyn | Tyn | Tyrel |
| Twynn | Tynan | Tyrell |
| Ty | Tyndall | Tyron |
| Tyble | Tyne | Tyrone |
| Tycoon | Tyner | Tyrrell |
| Tye | Tynette | Tys |
| Tyee | Tynille | Tysen |
| | | Tyson |

U is for "Unique," that's what you are to me—
every ounce of you, my precious Baby.

| | | |
|---|---|---|
| Uba | Ulas | Underwood |
| Ubel | Ulen | Undine |
| Ubelaker | Ulhrika | Uness |
| Uben | Ulises | Ungren |
| Ubias | Ulissa | Unich |
| Ucol | Ulla | Union |
| Udall | Ullin | Unique |
| Udarov | Ullma | Unit |
| Udel | Ulma | Unita |
| Uganda | Ulna | Unity |
| Ugo | Ulrich | Universal |
| Uhlmeyer | Ulrick | Universe |
| Uilenberg | Ulrika | University |
| Uka | Ultra | Up |
| Ukel | Ulysses | Upala |
| Ukiah | Uma | Upana |
| Ukraine | Umak | Uphana |
| Ula | Umayama | Upland |
| Ulak | Umayma | Upmeyer |
| Ulan | Umber | Upshaw |
| Ularia | Umbria | Upson |
| Ularov | Una | Upton |

Urban
Urdrian
Ureka
Urena
Uri
Uriah
Urich
Uriel
Urmi
Urquhart
Ursa

Ursel
Ursie
Ursola
Ursula
Ursulina
Ursy
Uruguay
Usaid
Use
Ush
Usher

Usoro
Utah
Utak
Utheim
Utica
Utility
Utilize
Uvalda
Uwem
Uy
Uznanski
Uzunow

V is for "Virtues" (loyalty, kindness, obedience, truthfulness, integrity), a must in our lives. If you learn all of these you'll be very wise!

| | | |
|---|---|---|
| Vaagen | Vale | Vallary |
| Vacuum | Valencia | Valle |
| Vada | Valenda | Valley |
| Vade | Valenna | Valleyanne |
| Vaden | Valentin | Vallie |
| Vadim | Valentina | Vallonia |
| Vadin | Valentine | Vally |
| Vagas | Valentino | Valma |
| Vagen | Valenzuela | Valmay |
| Vahl | Valera | Valmont |
| Vaiant | Valere | Valor |
| Vaier | Valeria | Valora |
| Vail | Valerie | Valorie |
| Vakarro | Valery | Valsetz |
| Val | Valeta | Valu |
| Valaree | Valid | Value |
| Valarie | Valida | Vammen |
| Valatie | Valik | Vamoose |
| Valdez | Valina | Van |
| Valdivia | Valinda | Vanantwerp |
| Valdoma | Valkyrie | Vanassche |
| Valdosta | Valla | Vanberkom |

| | | |
|---|---|---|
| Vanbre | Vanssyckle | Vector |
| Vanbria | Vantage | Veda |
| Vanbuskirk | Vanwey | Veden |
| Vance | Vanzandt | Vedis |
| Vand | Vanzant | Veenstra |
| Vanda | Vara | Vega |
| Vander | Varen | Vegas |
| Vanderpool | Vareniki | Veikko |
| Vanderstaay | Varenka | Velarde |
| Vanderwaal | Varese | Velasco |
| Vanderzouwen | Vargo | Velda |
| Vandewall | Variation | Veldez |
| Vandyk | Varietal | Veldhuizen |
| Vandyke | Variety | Veldonna |
| Vanern | Varina | Veleke |
| Vanesa | Varinka | Velez |
| Vanessa | Varnea | Velice |
| Vanguard | Varneá | Velinde |
| Vanhess | Varneé | Vella |
| Vanhomrigh | Varnez | Velma |
| Vanhorn | Varolo | Veloni |
| Vanhorne | Vashon | Velora |
| Vanhoven | Vashtar | Veloria |
| Vankirk | Vashti | Velour |
| Vanlund | Vass | Veltex |
| Vanmieghem | Vassar | Veltry |
| Vann | Vast | Velva |
| Vanna | Vatia | Velvet |
| Vannes | Vatter | Velvetum |
| Vannex | Vaughan | Velvina |
| Vanny | Vaughn | Velvor |
| Vanora | Vazquez | Vena |
| Vanoss | Veach | Venable |
| Vanparys | Vead | Venateire |

| | | |
|---|---|---|
| Venee | Verine | Vertz |
| Venesa | Veritable | Verus |
| Venessa | Verity | Veryl |
| Venet | Verl | Ves |
| Venetta | Verla | Vesam |
| Venezuela | Verlie | Vesper |
| Venice | Verlin | Vess |
| Venio | Verlon | Vessel |
| Venisha | Vermont | Vessey |
| Venison | Vern | Vessie |
| Venizia | Verna | Vessy |
| Vennetta | Vernadine | Vest |
| Vensel | Verne | Vesta |
| Ventron | Vernell | Vestal |
| Ventura | Verner | Vester |
| Venture | Vernetta | Vet |
| Venturei | Vernette | Vett |
| Venus | Vernice | Vetter |
| Veny | Vernie | Vi |
| Vera | Vernier | Vian |
| Veranda | Vernon | Vianca |
| Verb | Vero | Viand |
| Verda | Verona | Vianey |
| Verdel | Veronica | Viasa |
| Verdi | Veronika | Viatricia |
| Verdie | Veronique | Vic |
| Verdon | Verral | Vicar |
| Vereb | Verranda | Vice |
| Verena | Versá | Vicenta |
| Verene | Versal | Vicente |
| Vergie | Verse | Vickey |
| Vergil | Versie | Vicki |
| Verify | Vertheen | Vickie |
| Verina | Vertu | Vicky |

| | | |
|---|---|---|
| Vicount | Vina | Virello |
| Victoire | Vinateire | Virgie |
| Victor | Vince | Virgil |
| Victoria | Vincent | Virginia |
| Victorine | Vincenza | Virgo |
| Victory | Vincenzo | Virtu |
| Vida | Vine | Virtue |
| Vidal | Vineeta | Virtuette |
| Viderids | Vines | Visa |
| Vidette | Vinetari | Visalia |
| Viduuds | Vinette | Visi |
| Vienna | Ving | Vision |
| Vierena | Vinh | Vista |
| Vierra | Vinnie | Vistant |
| Viesselman | Vinod | Vit |
| View | Vins | Vita |
| Viewer | Vinson | Vitas |
| Viggo | Vintage | Vito |
| Viglaski | Vintar | Vitoria |
| Vigna | Vintari | Vitte |
| Vike | Vinter | Vitti |
| Viken | Vintilo | Viv |
| Viking | Vinton | Viva |
| Vikki | Vinyl | Viveca |
| Viktor | Viola | Viveka |
| Viktoria | Violante | Vivian |
| Vila | Viole | Viviana |
| Vilas | Violet | Vivien |
| Vileta | Violete | Vivienne |
| Vilhelmina | Violetta | Vivita |
| Vilim | Violette | Vivus |
| Village | Vira | Vivyen |
| Villarreal | Virag | Vizena |
| Vilma | Virdalene | Vizzini |

Vocal
Vogt
Voigtsberger
Volanda
Volk
Volland
Volmette
Volosen
Volta
Volume
Von
Vonda
Vondran

Vonieta
Vonney
Vonnie
Vonny
Voorhees
Vor
Vorass
Vorenkamp
Vorn
Vorwerk
Voss
Vosse
Voth

Vouvray
Vowel
Vowels
Voyage
Vranna
Vreeland
Vrijeda
Vuarnet
Vuong
Vy
Vylvana
Vyvian

W is for the "Whys" that may drive us up the wall,
and for the Wisdom it takes to answer them all!

| | | |
|---|---|---|
| Wabash | Waine | Wale |
| Wabbey | Waino | Wales |
| Wabbit | Wainwright | Walesea |
| Wac | Wait | Waleska |
| Wach | Waite | Walgamott |
| Waco | Waiter | Waligorski |
| Wact | Waitte | Walk |
| Wade | Wake | Walker |
| Waden | Wakefall | Walkin |
| Wader | Wakefield | Walking |
| Wadleigh | Waken | Wall |
| Wadsworth | Wakena | Wallaby |
| Wag | Waker | Wallace |
| Wagemann | Wakjira | Wallaia |
| Wagen | Wal | Wallbert |
| Waggoner | Walbert | Wallen |
| Wagner | Walch | Waller |
| Wagnur | Wald | Walli |
| Wagon | Waldemar | Wallie |
| Wagoner | Walden | Wallis |
| Wahlman | Waldo | Walls |
| Wain | Waldron | Wally |

| | | |
|---|---|---|
| Wallys | Warrick | Waverly |
| Walmart | Warring | Waves |
| Walmarty | Warrington | Wavrin |
| Walsh | Wartes | Wax |
| Walston | Warwich | Waxie |
| Walt | Warwick | Way |
| Walter | Wash | Wayan |
| Walters | Washabaugh | Wayat |
| Walton | Washburn | Waylan |
| Wanda | Washington | Wayland |
| Wander | Wasim | Waylen |
| Wandis | Wasmundt | Waylon |
| Waneta | Wass | Wayman |
| Wanita | Wassail | Waymen |
| Wanna | Wasson | Waymer |
| Wanter | Wat | Waymon |
| Wanton | Watanabe | Wayne |
| Ward | Watch | Ways |
| Wardell | Watcher | Wayt |
| Warder | Wate | Wayward |
| Ware | Water | We |
| Wareing | Waterman | Wealth |
| Warfield | Waters | Wear |
| Wargo | Wates | Weary |
| Wariel | Watkins | Weather |
| Waring | Watkinson | Weatherby |
| Warm | Watson | Weatherford |
| Warmer | Watt | Weathers |
| Warne | Watte | Weave |
| Warnecke | Watts | Weaver |
| Warner | Watzit | Webb |
| Warnes | Waud | Webber |
| Warren | Wava | Weber |
| Warrenton | Wave | Webster |

| | | |
|---|---|---|
| Wed | Wellington | West |
| Weddle | Wells | West Virginia |
| Wedeman | Wellsandt | Westbay |
| Wednesday | Welsh | Westby |
| Weed | Welt | Westcote |
| Weedy | Welton | Westcott |
| Weeks | Welty | Westen |
| Weese | Wenatchee | Western |
| Wege | Wenberg | Westfall |
| Weger | Wendee | Westfield |
| Wegner | Wendeline | Westin |
| Wehbe | Wendell | Westley |
| Wehmeyer | Wendi | Westling |
| Wei | Wending | Westlund |
| Weiblen | Wendlandt | Westman |
| Weida | Wendling | Westom |
| Weidman | Wendolyn | Weston |
| Weigand | Wendy | Westport |
| Weigel | Wenger | Wet |
| Weigh | Wensley | Weyand |
| Weil | Wentworth | Weyburn |
| Weiler | Wentz | Weyerts |
| Wein | Wenz | Wezenberg |
| Weir | Wenzyl | Whale |
| Weiss | Wepfer | Whalen |
| Weitz | Werda | Whaler |
| Wel | Werner | Whaley |
| Welch | Wernett | Whalton |
| Welcome | Wes | Whaylen |
| Weld | Wescott | Whayton |
| Welder | Wesel | Wheat |
| Weldon | Wesley | Wheather |
| Welfare | Weslyn | Wheaton |
| Welland | Wesson | Whee |

Wheel
Wheeler
Whell
When
Where
Wherry
Whether
Which
Whidbey
Whigham
Whipple
Whisker
Whiskey
Whisky
Whisp
Whisper
Whistle
Whistler
Whit
Whitacre
Whitaker
White
Whitehouse
Whitey
Whitfield
Whitford
Whither
Whiting
Whitley
Whitlock
Whitman
Whitmore
Whitney
Whitson

Whittaker
Whittock
Whity
Wholeman
Whoopi
Whoopie
Whyte
Wichita
Wichman
Wick
Wickett
Wickland
Wicks
Wickson
Widen
Wiebe
Wiemer
Wienholz
Wiens
Wiersma
Wieslawa
Wiggens
Wiggers
Wiggin
Wiggles
Wight
Wikan
Wil
Wilander
Wilann
Wilber
Wilbert
Wilbour
Wilbur

Wilburn
Wilconson
Wilcox
Wild
Wilda
Wilder
Wilderness
Wildman
Wildon
Wiletta
Wiley
Wilfolour
Wilford
Wilfred
Wilfredo
Wilfrid
Wilhelm
Wilhelma
Wilhelmi
Wilhelmina
Wilhelmine
Wilke
Wilkens
Wilkerson
Wilkes
Wilkey
Wilkin
Wilkins
Wilkinson
Will
Willa
Willabelle
Willamena
Willand

Willanne
Willard
Willemyn
Willene
Willett
Willetta
Willette
Willia
William
Williams
Williamson
Willian
Willie
Willing
Willis
Willms
Willodenia
Willoughby
Willow
Willowby
Wills
Willson
Willy
Wilma
Wilmer
Wilmore
Wilson
Wilt
Wilton
Win
Winchell
Winchester
Wind
Windell

Winden
Windie
Windle
Windmill
Window
Windred
Windsong
Windsor
Windy
Wine
Wines
Winfield
Winford
Winfred
Winfrey
Wing
Winge
Winger
Wingler
Wings
Winifred
Winje
Winkle
Winkler
Winkley
Winn
Winner
Winnie
Winnifred
Winningham
Winnow
Winny
Winoma
Winona

Winside
Winsley
Winslow
Winsom
Winsome
Winsong
Winston
Winstone
Winter
Winters
Winto
Winton
Wire
Wirkkala
Wirtanen
Wirto
Wisconsin
Wisdom
Wise
Wiseman
Wisen
Wish
Wishin
Wishing
Wisner
Wison
Wisp
Wisper
Wiss
Wissing
Wistful
Wit
Witecki
Withrow

Wixson
Wlazlak
Wm
Wocken
Wofford
Wohlfrom
Wohlsein
Wojciechowski
Wold
Wolf
Wolfe
Wolff
Wolffe
Wolfgang
Wolley
Wollfe
Wolosyn
Womack
Won
Wonch
Wonder
Woo
Wood
Woodbury
Wooden
Woodley
Woodrow

Woodruff
Woods
Woodward
Woody
Wool
Woolen
Worcester
Worden
Worgum
Work
World
Wornell
Worrell
Worth
Wottlin
Wrangler
Wrap
Wrath
Wrigh
Wright
Wriston
Writer
Wry
Wu
Wudan
Wunder
Wutzke

Wuz
Wuzzy
Wyan
Wyann
Wyatt
Wyeth
Wyett
Wyle
Wyler
Wyley
Wylie
Wylma
Wyman
Wynalda
Wynands
Wynne
Wynona
Wynsong
Wyoming
Wyomy
Wyre
Wyrick
Wyse
Wyson
Wysong
Wyss

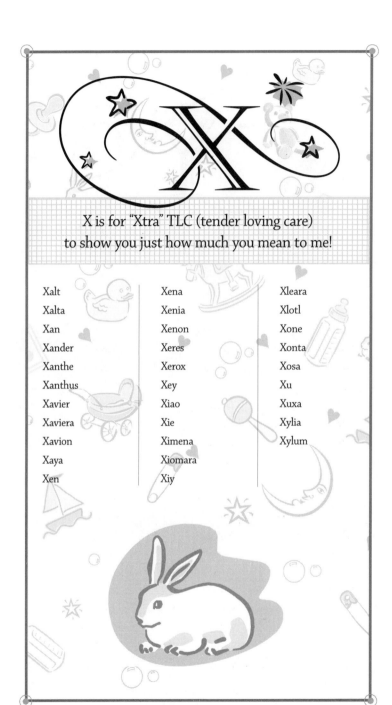

# X

X is for "Xtra" TLC (tender loving care)
to show you just how much you mean to me!

| | | |
|---|---|---|
| Xalt | Xena | Xleara |
| Xalta | Xenia | Xlotl |
| Xan | Xenon | Xone |
| Xander | Xeres | Xonta |
| Xanthe | Xerox | Xosa |
| Xanthus | Xey | Xu |
| Xavier | Xiao | Xuxa |
| Xaviera | Xie | Xylia |
| Xavion | Ximena | Xylum |
| Xaya | Xiomara | |
| Xen | Xiy | |

Y is for "You're so cute" and "You're all mine."
You're my sweet little Valentine!

| | | |
|---|---|---|
| Yabal | Yamada | Yared |
| Yach | Yamaguchi | Yaritza |
| Yacht | Yamanda | Yarn |
| Yacob | Yamim | Yarow |
| Yacoub | Yamina | Yarrow |
| Yadira | Yamma | Yarrows |
| Yael | Yampa | Yas |
| Yafa | Yan | Yasha |
| Yafah | Yanah | Yasiman |
| Yager | Yancey | Yasin |
| Yahaira | Yanez | Yasir |
| Yair | Yanira | Yasmeen |
| Yajaira | Yanis | Yasmin |
| Yak | Yankauskas | Yasmine |
| Yakima | Yantas | Yasseen |
| Yakina | Yantis | Yasuda |
| Yaklich | Yantz | Yate |
| Yaksic | Yarah | Yates |
| Yal | Yarboro | Yaurdley |
| Yalath | Yard | Yazid |
| Yale | Yarden | Yazmin |
| Yallow | Yardley | Ybarra |

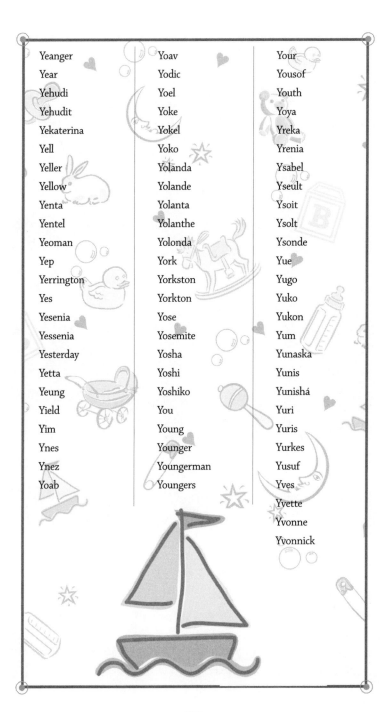

Yeanger
Year
Yehudi
Yehudit
Yekaterina
Yell
Yeller
Yellow
Yenta
Yentel
Yeoman
Yep
Yerrington
Yes
Yesenia
Yessenia
Yesterday
Yetta
Yeung
Yield
Yim
Ynes
Ynez
Yoab

Yoav
Yodic
Yoel
Yoke
Yokel
Yoko
Yolanda
Yolande
Yolanta
Yolanthe
Yolonda
York
Yorkston
Yorkton
Yose
Yosemite
Yosha
Yoshi
Yoshiko
You
Young
Younger
Youngerman
Youngers

Your
Yousof
Youth
Yoya
Yreka
Yrenia
Ysabel
Yseult
Ysoit
Ysolt
Ysonde
Yue
Yugo
Yuko
Yukon
Yum
Yunaska
Yunis
Yunishá
Yuri
Yuris
Yurkes
Yusuf
Yves
Yvette
Yvonne
Yvonnick

Z is for "Zippy" that you can be.
You buzz around like a busy little bee!

| | | |
|---|---|---|
| Zab | Zahara | Zale |
| Zabel | Zaharra | Zales |
| Zabes | Zaharris | Zalesky |
| Zabiaka | Zahira | Zally |
| Zabika | Zahl | Zalma |
| Zabrina | Zahn | Zalman |
| Zabriskie | Zahran | Zambara |
| Zac | Zahren | Zambas |
| Zace | Zaid | Zameria |
| Zach | Zaida | Zamoia |
| Zachariah | Zain | Zamora |
| Zacharias | Zaira | Zan |
| Zachary | Zaire | Zana |
| Zachery | Zaitoun | Zandell |
| Zack | Zajac | Zander |
| Zackary | Zajek | Zandra |
| Zackery | Zak | Zandria |
| Zada | Zakary | Zane |
| Zade | Zakel | Zaneta |
| Zadee | Zakelina | Zanna |
| Zagora | Zaki | Zanzibar |
| Zagreb | Zako | Zap |

| | | |
|---|---|---|
| Zapata | Zebulon | Zenas |
| Zaphod | Zecca | Zenda |
| Zappa | Zechariah | Zenevieva |
| Zara | Zed | Zenia |
| Zaragoza | Zedland | Zenith |
| Zarah | Zee | Zeniveev |
| Zarak | Zeeland | Zenker |
| Zard | Zeeman | Zenner |
| Zared | Zehner | Zeno |
| Zarek | Zeigler | Zent |
| Zarelli | Zeke | Zepha |
| Zariah | Zelasko | Zephyr |
| Zarina | Zelda | Zepp |
| Zarita | Zeldenrust | Zer |
| Zavanna | Zeleka | Zerelda |
| Zavella | Zelia | Zero |
| Zavid | Zelinski | Zeth |
| Zawistowski | Zeliss | Zetta |
| Zaysy | Zelissa | Zeus |
| Zazu | Zell | Zev |
| Zdar | Zella | Zevenbergen |
| Zea | Zeller | Zevi |
| Zeá | Zellissa | Zeze |
| Zeal | Zelma | Zhang |
| Zealand | Zelous | Zhivago |
| Zealot | Zemball | Zia |
| Zeandra | Zembel | Ziara |
| Zear | Zemen | Zie |
| Zearing | Zemlya | Ziegler |
| Zeb | Zemora | Ziela |
| Zebe | Zemorah | Ziele |
| Zebedee | Zen | Zielinski |
| Zebedy | Zena | Ziella |
| Zeben | Zenah | Zieman |

| | | |
|---|---|---|
| Zier | Ziyad | Zucati |
| Zigler | Zoar | Zueger |
| Zigmund | Zoe | Zuidweg |
| Zillah | Zoey | Zukowski |
| Zillie | Zofia | Zula |
| Zillyette | Zohowski | Zulma |
| Zilvia | Zoie | Zumbrota |
| Zimbalist | Zoila | Zung |
| Zimmer | Zola | Zuni |
| Zimmeranne | Zoline | Zuniga |
| Zimmerman | Zoller | Zuri |
| Zina | Zoltan | Zurich |
| Zinc | Zomora | Zuriel |
| Zindell | Zona | Zuwena |
| Zink | Zonal | Zuzanna |
| Zinnia | Zone | Zuzanny |
| Zinque | Zonta | Zuzeth |
| Zion | Zoo | Zuzi |
| Zip | Zophia | Zuzu |
| Zipper | Zora | Zvean |
| Zira | Zoraida | Zven |
| Zirah | Zorintha | Zvi |
| Zircon | Zoro | Zvie |
| Zirk | Zosia | Zvono |
| Zirkle | Zozi | Zyana |
| Zirl | Zsa Zsa | Zygar |
| Zita | Zuba | Zylan |
| Zito | Zubb | Zync |
| Ziv | Zube | Zynk |

# PREGNANCY
# JOURNAL

I remember during my early pregnancy that I couldn't find any journals for expectant mothers, so I had to create my own. There were so many things at the time I wanted to write down so I wouldn't forget!

I've included a great little diary where you can keep notes of special things. I guarantee you'll be glad you did, and you can show your child when he or she is older.

★ Memories, feelings, cravings, morning sickness, swelling, doctor visits, first kick, labor pains, how long until delivery, your favorite nurse

★ Certain foods/smells you love or hate

★ Themes you chose for the nursery

★ How much weight you gained (scratch that one)

★ Names picked out monthly (I kept changing my mine)

Included in the pages that follow is a place for baby's ultrasound pictures to go along with yours. I wish I'd taken more pictures during each stage of my pregnancies.

So get with it and start snapping that camera and taking notes! Nine months fly by before you know it, and for some it might even be sooner. Enjoy and have fun. God bless each one of you and your babies!

—MARTY

# Notes

Belly Pics

1st month

# Notes

Belly Pics

2nd month

# Notes

Belly Pics

3rd month

*Notes*

Baby Pics

# Notes

Belly Pics

4th month

# Notes

Belly Pics

5th month

# Notes

Belly Pics

6th month

_Notes_

Belly Pics

7th month

# Notes

Baby Pics

# Notes

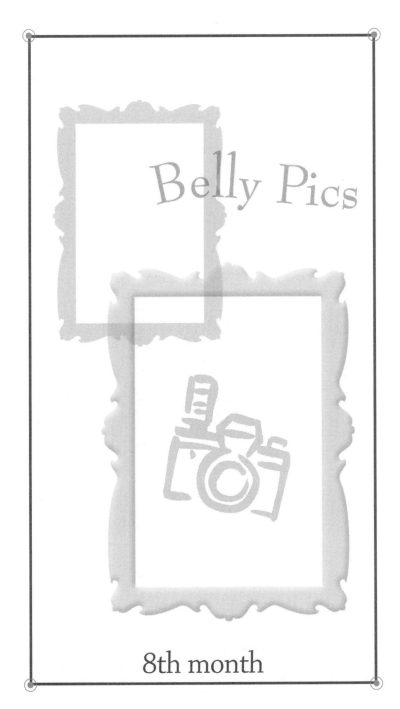

Belly Pics

8th month

# Notes

Belly Pics

9th month

*Notes*

*Notes*

Notes

# Notes

# Notes

*Notes*

# Notes

TO ORDER

Mail: 80 East Ridgecrest Drive, Union, WA 98592

Phone: 888-660-0277

Fax: 360-898-7003

E-mail: Martykwilson@aol.com

Book Price: $19.99

plus Shipping & Handling $3.95

Ask about multiple book discounts

## About the Author

MARTY WILSON was born, raised, and still resides in the Pacific Northwest. She's owned several styling salons throughout the course of thirty years, but her first love is sharing activities with her wonderful husband Brad, along with her daughter Season, and her two sons, Story and Salem.

Marty uses a lot of her time being creative as both an author and an artist, and also enjoys fishing, golfing, traveling, and spending time with her family and friends. She's a devoted Christian and believes that all our gifts in life are blessings from God.